Germany, Austria & Switzerland

Short Stay Guide

Germany, Austria & Switzerland

Little Hills Press

Text by Fay Smith and LHP Editorial Staff
©Little Hills Press, February 2002

Editor and designer: Mark Truman
Publisher: Charles Burfitt

Printed in China

Germany, Austria & Switzerland
Short Stay Guide
ISBN 1 86315 198 2

Little Hills Press
Sydney, Australia
www.littlehills.com
info@littlehills.com

All rights reserved. No part of this publication may be reproduced, stored in a retrieval system, or transmitted in any form or by any means, electronic, mechanical, photocopying, recording or otherwise, without the prior permission in writing of the publisher.

DISCLAIMER
Whilst all care has been taken by the publisher and authors to ensure that the information is accurate and up to date, the publisher does not take responsibility for the information published herein or the consequences of its use. The recommendations are those of the writing team, and as things get better or worse, with places closing and others opening, some elements in the book may be inaccurate when you arrive. Please inform us of any discrepancies so that we can update subsequent editions.

Little Hills™ and are registered trademarks of Little Hills Press Pty Ltd.

Contents

Preface

How To Use this Book 9

Part One

Introduction 11

Part Two

Germany 35
   Berlin 38
   Bonn 52
   Cologne 54
   Frankfurt am Main 60
   Heidelberg 68
   Munich 70
   Black Forest 78
   Driving Through Germany 79

Austria 83
   Vienna 87
   Salzburg 97
   Innsbruck 105
   Driving Through Austria 107

Switzerland 109
   Lucerne 112
   Zurich 120

Bern 129
Geneva 131
Interlaken 133
Driving Through Switzerland 134

Part Three

Index 137

Preface

WELCOME TO GERMANY, Austria and Switzerland! These amazing countries are made up of many landscapes, each with its own particular identity. Every city and town has a rich history and will provide you with unique experiences never to be forgotten.

Reunited only twelve years ago, the capital of Germany, Berlin, has a history of hardship and is undergoing many changes. Here you can see the broken remnants of the famous wall and pass through the Brandenburg Gate. In Bonn, walk through the pleasant streets of this charming city and visit the birthplace of Beethoven. Cologne has its huge cathedral, set against the forefront of the Rhine River. The financial centre of Frankfurt am Main has its skyscrapers, including Europe's tallest office building, the Commerzbank. Take an afternoon amble down the cobblestone paths of Heidelberg, a university town that attracts visitors, particularly Americans, like moths to a flame. Frequent the local beer halls of the Bavarian capital, Munich. Enjoy the stunning scenery of the Black Forest, from its cascading waterfalls to the foreboding woods, on a hike or a drive.

In Vienna, stroll along the Danube, hear the Vienna Boys' Choir, watch the Lippizaner stallions go through their paces in the Hofburg, or take a day trip to the breathtaking Schonbrunn Palace. Fans will want to take the Sound of Music tour in Salzburg, while others will head up to the amazing Hohensalzburg Fortress, or admire the city cathedral in all its Renaissance splendour. Hemmed in by snow-capped alpine peaks, the famous town of Innsbruck welcomes its visitors with fresh air and quaint medieval streets.

In Lucerne, camera-bearers will want to capture the fourteenth century Wasserturm and Kapellbrucke structures on film, then find themselves moved, as Mark Twain did, by the Dying Lion Monument. Zurich has its landmark Grossmunster, the Swiss National Museum, and the cultural icons of the Opera House and Schauspielhaus theatre. Bern, Switzerland's riverside capital, offers visitors its beautifully preserved medieval Old Town. The country's banking centre, Geneva, is set attractively on the edge of Lake Geneva. Interlaken, situated in central Switzerland, is a haven for visitors in summer, who explore the surrounding alpine peaks, undertake adventure sports in the valley rivers or take an unforgettable day trip up to the summit of Jungfrau.

There is a place in Germany, Austria and Switzerland to appeal to every traveller.

This book is designed for people who plan to visit particular cities and regions, whether or not they are on a whirlwind tour. It assumes that you do not have a lot of time in these places, and provides thorough details of their main attractions so that you can head directly to the spots that interest you most. It therefore lists what are in our opinion the most important sights to see.

Some may prefer to rise in the morning at their leisure, spend some time getting to know the local scene, the people and the attractions, then find their favourite restaurant, club or park, or a delightful little

bookshop where they can browse endlessly. The pace of your holiday is completely dependent on you.

We have developed suggested tours for you to undertake on foot. Whilst exploring the cities and towns of Germany, Austria and Switzerland, cars are really an encumberance, even in a vast city such as Berlin, where it is best to take advantage of the trains and then hail a taxi if necessary. Going on foot with a light rucksack means that you are more flexible and can adapt your plans without unnecessary hassles, such as finding parking, paying for parking, having to return to the car constantly whenever you wish to move on, and worrying about it being broken into or damaged while you are away.

How To Use This Book

Symbols

Throughout the text you will find that symbols have been used to denote the information that follows, whether it be an admission price, opening time, phone number, email or web address. This will aid you in locating the specific details you desire more quickly.

Here is a list of the symbols used with an explanation of each:

- ℂ indicates a phone number
- ✪ indicates a price
- ⏱ indicates opening times
- 👁 indicates a web site
- ✎ indicates an email address

Accommodation and Eating Out

The *Accommodation* and *Food and Drink* sections contain by no means an exhaustive list of what each city has to offer. We have tried to cater for a range of tastes and provide suggestions for your selection. Places listed are designed to give you a basis for comparison and to act at the very least as a starting point for the planning of your holiday. All budgets from lavish to limited have been considered and included.

Taxes

Where possible we have included the tax for a specific service. For example, a 15% VAT is included in the price of most consumables in Germany. In restaurants, a tip of a couple of Deutschmarks is acceptable if the service has been good. Switzerland has high prices but a VAT of only 6.5%, and tips are not expected, though they are obviously appreciated. In contrast, Austria has a VAT between 20% and 34% on selected items.

Maps

Before you begin your trip, we suggest that you purchase comprehensive maps of the cities you intend to visit - ones that include as much detail of the streets, avenues and alleys as possible. Guidebooks, because of space restrictions, usually provide less detail and seek to give visitors their bearings and a general overview of the city's layout. For the serious traveller, such maps will not suffice and shouldn't be relied upon. In a foreign city you want to be able to pinpoint your location as accurately as possible, to improve your sightseeing efficiency and to ensure that you do not miss anything. A good map will also come in handy if you find yourself a little lost after an intrepid stroll. In addition, if you plan to tour an entire country, perhaps by car, a thorough road map is essential.

Internet Information

For your convenience you will find throughout this book relevant websites and email addresses, which can be used for the preliminary planning of your holiday in Germany, Austria and Switzerland.

PART ONE

Introduction

THIS CHAPTER OUTLINES some travel tips which you may find helpful. Specific details for each city or town, including local transport, shopping, accommodation, food and sightseeing, are contained in each section devoted to the particular areas we have covered.

Passport

You need a passport to travel. For first time travellers the following are some of the documents required before you can be issued with a passport - birth certificate and/or proof of citizenship, photographs of which at least two are passport-size, your drivers' license and so on. Normally you will have a face-to-face interview with a government official.

Generally speaking you are looking at paying over A$130 (US$65) for a passport valid for 10 years. In most cases passports are valid for 10 years, however they are useless if they have less than 6 months left on them unless you are an Australian going to New Zealand and vice versa. This does not apply to any other countries.

Here are some important contacts who will tell you exactly what you need and where to lodge the application:

Australia: 　　　　📞131232
　　　　　　　　👁www.dfat.gov.au/passports
Canada: 　　　　　📞800 567 6868
　　　　　　　　👁www.dfait-maeci.gc.ca/passport/passport.htm
New Zealand: 　　📞0800 225 050
　　　　　　　　fax 64 4 748 010
　　　　　　　　👁www.passports.govt.nz/
United Kingdom: 📞0870 521 0410
　　　　　　　　👁www.ukpa.gov.uk
USA: 　　　　　　📞1 900 225 5674 or 1 888 362 8668
　　　　　　　　👁www.travel.state.gov

Money

Some of us still like to have a few travellers cheques just in case, however the way of the present is the credit card or the bank card, which you can activate at any ATM in most cities in Germany, Austria and Switzerland.

If you have a credit card make sure it also has a pin number. This may seem like a superfluous comment, however some credit cards are only secured by a password, which is useless if the ATM in Germany, Austria or Switzerland requires you to enter a pin number for your card.

Make sure the account your card accesses is cashed up before you travel. Also check to see if the money is accessible before you leave, just in case the bank or the financial organisation you deal with has made a mistake or is suffering technical problems. Try making a simple withdrawal and check the balance.

You might like to get the phone numbers you will need to call if you have credit card hassles in each of the countries you plan to visit. If you want to, test them from home before you leave. At night it will probably cost you $2 in total and save you making frantic calls to dead ends in the unfortunate event that a problem arises.

Web Sites for the Major Credit Cards

These sites can provide you with the location of offices and ATMs in Germany, Austria and Switzerland.

- www.americanexpress.com.au/atm/atm.asp
- www.thomascook.com (a confusing site but you may be able to find your way around it)
- www.mastercard.com/atm
- www.visa.com/pd/atm/main.html

When changing money at either a bank or a Bureau de Change it is important to check the commission fee to avoid being overcharged. Ask beforehand or check the notices near the counter carefully (look for the fine print!). Fees should be no more than a few marks.

Make sure you always keep the receipts. If you are heading into Germany, Austria or Switzerland from another European country or vice versa, and you want to change your money from the currency of one country to that of your destination, you will invariably be asked to produce a receipt to prove that you purchased the currency whilst in the country you are in. If you cannot show the receipt you will be denied.

Contact Details and Valuables

The following tip is something that any travel agent and decent guidebook will advise.

It is worthwhile to have two copies of each of the documents listed on the following page.

- Passport - the front two pages which have your identification details and photograph, and also pages where Visas appear.

Part of the Swiss Alps

- Your ticket/s
- Driver's license
- Insurance documentation
- Travellers Cheque numbers
- Credit Card details - just the numbers, not any identifying marks showing what card it is. Write them in a jumbled up way that doesn't look specific except to you.

Put these at the bottom of your suitcase where you will hopefully not see them until you return and unpack your bags. Forget about them for now. If you need them you will know where to find them.

Leave the second lot of copies with family back home. This will save you a lot of problems if disaster strikes.

Insurance

It is advisable to take out comprehensive insurance for the duration of your stay. Your travel agent can handle this for you and it normally covers you for loss of personal belongings, specific flight cancellations or rerouting, medical costs including all hospital and doctors' fees and any emergency transport associated with this, injury, and death (not suicide). Payment is made for the number of days you are away. Of course, the rates vary as does the coverage, so shop around.

Driving Through Germany, Austria and Switzerland

Camper vans and mobile homes (RVs in the US) are common throughout Europe. Using one makes it obvious that you are a tourist, not only by the number plate. It is a convenient way to travel but be warned that when you leave the vehicle it can become a target for thieves, since the theory is that travelling tourists have their valuables centred in one place: the vehicle. So it is a good idea to have your passport, credit cards and money on you. Any other valuables you do not plan to take with you should be hidden somewhere in the vehicle and not exposed if someone peers through the window.

Some people opt for a van or a station wagon, in which they can put a fold-down mattress. These are not obvious tourist vehicles and so may have less chance of being tamperered with, although in some cities it is essential to hide everything from view regardless of the type of vehicle, otherwise a break-in is guaranteed.

Remember, in budgeting for travelling around Germany, Austria and Switzerland, you should keep in mind the cost of fuel in your different ports of call. As a rule of thumb the country areas will be more expensive than the city. Diesel will be more expensive per gallon or litre but will take you much further per litre or gallon and is more efficient.

Trains

Eurail is one way to book and organise your tickets. It allows you to develop some flexibility with regard to where you want to travel. In addition to the basic travel component of the fare you must pay an additional charge for your individual seat. Depending on the country and the type of train, seats must be booked in advance, although this is not always necessary and you should check first.

The two web sites listed below have good information and allow you to book and pay online.

Rail Pass Express: 👁 www.eurail.com
RailEurope: 👁 www.raileurope.com (info and commercial)
Die Bahn: 👁 www.bahn.de

Note that if you travel at off peak times the prices are much cheaper. This is especially the case if you book a certain number of days in advance. If you are going to be there for a week or so and plan to do a lot of travel by train, enquire at the rail information centres for their special passes giving you cheaper fares.

Taxis

Public transport in Germany, Austria and Switzerland is generally good, once you learn to navigate it. However, there almost always comes a time when a taxi is required to fill in a gap or to avoid rain. Taxi fares in Germany, Austria and Switzerland are by no means cheap. Berlin is expensive; a trip within the city can cost the equivalent of $19 US dollars (A$35). For comparison, a 10 kilometre trip in Zurich will cost you more than US$21 (A$40), while in Vienna a journey of the same distance will cost about US$12 (A$23).

If you have the option of using either the U-Bahn or S-Bahn systems, take it.

Most taxis do not accept credit cards, so you should assume that cabs require cash.

It can sometimes occur that your hotel is not far from the station or airport where you have just arrived - but it is raining and the distance is too far to cart your luggage. If you are in the queue and discover that the drivers are enquiring about your destination then waving you away and moving onto the next person, it is because you do not have a decent fare to offer them. Should you find yourself in a similar situation, head into the street and hail a taxi - once you are settled comfortably inside with all your gear, break the news to the driver in a confident, matter-of-fact tone.

Force yourself to shrug off the travel fatigue and have presence of mind when you arrive in a new city. Watch what the locals are doing - it may take some minutes - but you will soon find the nearest taxi stand and line up like everyone else.

Buses

Bus systems complement the efficient rail services in each of the three countries, and they are not excessively priced. In Lucerne it costs less than 2 Swiss francs to travel in one zone. A short trip in Munich costs less than DM2. In Salzburg you can get a day pass on the buses for about 20AS, the equivalent of US$2.60 (A$5).

What to Take

Germany, Austria and Switzerland, for Australians, United States citizens from southern California, and in fact anyone living below the 35th parallel, are cold and wet, particularly if you are travelling in January and February, when the temperatures drop to an average of -2C in Berlin and -3C in Vienna.

During winter, temperatures are not likely to climb above 10C in most places, and the rain is more prolific. Snow falls heavily in areas of high altitude. Daily temperatures in summer tend to hover in the low to mid twenties in many parts of the three countries. Neither Germany, Austria or Switzerland are subject to extreme weather.

The following items are certainly essential:

- A warm overcoat.
- A water and rain resistant coat including head cover - not one that is just damp resistant.
- An umbrella that you can fold up.
- A scarf.
- A hat or beanie, preferably one that covers the ears.

- A thick jumper (pullover).
- A winter suit (if you are going on business).
- Sturdy shoes - if you have a look at what you normally wear, they are probably thin soled leather shoes, or some sort of synthetic material that is not particularly thick. You may have to invest in a pair of thick soled shoes that will have you walking a couple of extra inches off the ground. As for pricing - check locally, and also whether they are water resistant.
- Walking shoes - a comfortable pair of well cushioned walking shoes are perfect for traversing the staggering number of cobblestone streets to be found throughout Europe. Level bitumen or beautiful soft grass is something apparently belonging only to the New World.
- Socks - warm and woollen.
- Gloves - indispensable.

If you are travelling throughout Europe in summer you can always dispense with the pullover and other bulky items, and wear shorts and a T-shirt instead.

Health

Fitness

It is hopeless to set off on this holiday without being in some sort of reasonable physical shape. It is a good idea to have a regular routine of physical exercise.

If you are going to be doing a lot of walking, and you should be, then before you go, walk every day or every second day for an hour or so, and do some other exercises that take care of the muscles in the back and the arms. Practice lifting by bending your knees, strengthening the muscles around your thighs, as you may have to cart your luggage for uncomfortable distances across arduous uphill terrain. Decide thoroughly what you must take and what are optional extras. Calculate the weight you will be carrying and remember: "If in doubt leave out". Younger travellers may find this a little amusing, but it is amazing how many 20 year olds suddenly find that they are out of shape and worse off than the oldies, believing that natural physique and youth will get them through. No matter what your age, if you do not do regular sport, start engaging in some regular exercise so you can develop the stamina to stay enthusiastic for the duration of your trip.

Adjusting

As far as some travellers are concerned, a trip to Germany, Austria and Switzerland is an endurance-test just to get there. Hours and hours in a plane is no fun, especially if you are not travelling business or first class. Even then, it is still something of an ordeal: change of time zones, disruption of sleeping patterns, and your tour begins the very day you arrive! After two weeks you are shuffling back onto a plane, heading home while suffering the flu and other related ailments - and this was a holiday?

Normally the adrenaline is pumping, but as you are so tired after the long flight, you will tend to sleep well on the first night. If you arrive in the day, try to stay up until nightfall and go to bed at a similar time, if not a little earlier, than is the local custom. Then the next day you should be ready for action. Force your victimised system to adjust and run on European time. That way you can take advantage of the daylight hours. This is a holiday, so the stress of a normal working day routine is absent - be vibrant, energetic, and enjoy.

Medicine

Your medicine bag should include those medicines you may not only need to take, but also those you may need in unforseen situations. The idea is to be prepared.

- Paracetomol
- Tinea cream
- Antiseptic
- Needle
- Cotton

- Tissues
- Tweezers
- Something for an upset stomach (One aunt of the contributors recommends half a glass of brandy followed by half a glass of port wine to cure an upset stomach).
- Ear plugs, for both the plane and hotel. They are also handy if you want to go swimming.

Remember that the old inhalation method can help a fluey cold. All you need for this is a towel, boiling water and a basin. Some may wish to add eucalyptus oil. Then get a good night's sleep and maybe a day's rest if necessary.

On the Plane

Sleeping

Most airlines do not give **eye patches** to economy class passengers on long haul flights. Exceptions to this are Qantas and British Airways. So take them with you. Ask your travel agent for a pair or ask where can you purchase them. A $3 purchase will be well worth it. For sleeping on long flights, eye patches are essential, otherwise your journey will feel that much longer and whatever sleep you do get will be at best fitful.

Some people prefer to use medicinal drugs, but there are at least a couple of good reasons to avoid them and try to get some natural sleep instead. Though the trip may seem shorter because you are out of it for hours, what happens when two hours after takeoff the plane needs to divert to another destination because of a minor problem with an O ring in the starboard engine? In your sleeping-pill induced stupor you must now attempt to clamber off the plane. Then there are the very rare cases when an emergency occurs. At such times you want to be at your most alert, especially if you need to disembark quickly. And we have not even mentioned the possible side effects. So avoid pills if you can.

An extra pair of socks may come in handy. Over extended periods of inaction, when you are riveted to your seat, your feet are likely to become targets for the plane's air-conditioning and will feel the cold most acutely. You want to preserve them for all that walking you will be doing once you touch down in Germany, Austria or Switzerland. Also, on a 13 hour flight sector, it is amazing how comfort becomes critically important among a person's priorities of survival.

Alcohol

Alcohol does not really help either. The constant air-conditioning dehydrates the body and you end up with swollen feet - try putting your shoes back on if you have not moved your feet for hours. Beer can have you running backwards and forwards to the smallest room on the plane - so if you want to have a few drinks, do your fellow passengers a favour and get a seat on the aisle.

Where to Sit

Fortunately now most airlines have a no smoking policy throughout the aircraft for long haul flights. For most travellers this development was not too soon coming. The bronchia's tend to end up less clogged on a flight where smoking is not permitted than on those with a smoking section. Watch out for this on European-owned airlines such as Alitalia. Also, European airlines tend to overbook and you may be shuffled into the smoking section if there are problems with seat allocation. Or you might end up in the smoking section because all the non-smoking seats are now occupied by a group of tourists on a package tour who booked four hours before you did. Since you only have a ruby frequent flyer card and not an emerald diamond, you will be ushered to the seat down the back next to the toilets. But you can't complain because you are lucky to have made the flight at all!

To try and avoid all this, it is best to have your seat allocated to you before you fly and make sure this is done for each leg or sector of your trip. If this cannot be achieved, try and check in early and see what the airline staff can do for you. It also helps to fly with an airline from your

River Main, Frankfurt

country of origin. They tend to realise that one benefit of accommodating you in Europe is that you might choose to fly with them domestically. After all, airlines developed frequent flyer programs precisely to give you that little extra perk which makes you feel important and persuades you to fly only with them. Use this marketing strategy to *your* advantage.

Give some consideration to where you prefer to be seated as it can contribute to being comfortable during the flight. Some people prefer to be seated in the back of the plane, others the front. The window is always the most popular. The emergency exit rows give you more leg room but you cannot spread out as the arms of the seats are fixed, whereas those in other rows can be moved up to increase your personal space. Also, in emergency exit rows luggage must be put in the overhead lockers, so you cannot have your carry-on luggage tucked into the pouch on the back of the seat in front of you for easy access. The aisle is fine as long as the person on the window or the middle does not get up too often during the flight. If you *are* stuck in the middle, politely ask the flight attendant if there is a chance you may be moved to either an aisle or a window seat. If not, console yourself with the thought that the flight will not last forever.

Airlines now advertise the pitch between the seats in economy class. Check these out, especially if you have long legs. This may determine your choice of airline, along with price, flight time to your destination, entertainment provided, and so on. Find out as much as you can about your intended airline and strive to tailor the flight to your needs.

Travel Agents

Booking on the web can be fine but certainly in the last couple of years travel agents have become much more professional - perhaps because they are competing with the web. Generally speaking they keep up-to-date by going on *famils* organised by airlines and travel wholesalers - the kinds of tour groups with whom you may end up. Some airlines see the agent as a vital link in their distribution channel. So when booking a flight or tour, the agent can put in a request for you; window seat, front of the plane, plenty of leg room, etc. An airline, if they can, will endeavour to accommodate the request. Agents can get good deals for you, sort out your wish list in half an hour and give you extra food for thought, whereas a convoluted web site may take a lot longer to navigate successfully. In addition, if you miss your flight they can put in a word for you and you may end up not having to pay a penalty fee. Remember that the web is closing in, but human contact remains alive and well.

Your Accommodation

It is important to set priorities based on your budget. Decide where you wish to splurge and give the credit card a work out at a luxurious four or five star hotel in the city centre, and where you will be content to stay in a comfortable, homely and relative inexpensive B&B on the outskirts of town.

The travel agent can book your accommodation for you. If you have no idea where to stay or the quality of accommodation that places offer, then get the travel agent to pursue this in detail for you. You can give your travel agent a budget and an idea of what sort of accommodation you want, what you expect from a hotel and where you want it to be located. A couple of extra dollars for a room will be more than compensated for by location, as you may not have to use public transport to reach the places you want to visit. Indeed, you will have more time for sightseeing if you are in the city centre.

This book gives you a range of hotels that vary in quality from excellent to ordinary, but all are clean and central. You can always go on the web and check out their prices there, or fax the hotel and ask for a quote, then compare this to what your agent can get for you. One thing about accommodation - try to get a room away from the street. Noise is a wonderful source of irritation for so many people.

It is a good idea to get the hotel reception to give you a wake up call - you're not here to sleep! Don't trust the alarm clock because both of you may be running on different time zones, and daylight saving may be a factor.

Web Addresses

To help familiarise yourself with Germany, Austria and Switzerland before you visit, we have included web addresses of the main official national tourism sites, plus a couple of others you may find useful, such as Eurail.

Austrian National Tourist Office ☜www.austria-tourism.at
German National Tourism Office ☜www.germany-tourism.de
Switzerland Tourism ☜www.myswitzerland.com

General Sites for Europe

Rail Pass Express ☜www.eurail.com
RailEurope ☜www.raileurope.com (info and commercial)
Europe Online ☜www.europeline.com
European Travel Commission ☜www.visiteurope.com

Kaiser Wilhelm Bad, Bad Homburg

Language
Here are 60+ words in German and French which should assist basic communication and may get you out of some trouble or help you to find your way around Germany, Austria and Switzerland.

German
Travel
airport	*flughafen*
bus	*bus*
railway station	*bahnhof*

taxi	*taxi*
ticket	*fahrkarte*

When you get there

bathroom	*baderzimmer*
beer	*bier*
chair	*sthul*
credit card	*kreditkarte*
elevator	*lift*
hotel	*hotel*
how much does it cost?	*wieviel kostet es?*
key	*schlüssel*
luggage	*gepäck*
my room	*ein zimmer*
restaurant	*ein restaurant, ein gaststätte*
street	*strasse*
table	*tisch*
to bed	*zo bett*
toilet	*toilette*
travel agency	*reisbüro*
wine	*wein*

Communicating

my name is...	*ich heisse..., mein name ist...*
excuse me please	*entschuldigung*
good evening	*guten abend*
good morning	*guten morgen*
goodbye	*auf wiedersehen*
hello	*guten tag, hallo*
I want	*Ich möchte*
I've a problem	*Ich habe problem*
no	*nein*
please	*bitte*
please help me	*bitte helfen*

sorry or pardon	*entschuldigung*
thank you	*danke*
this afternoon	*heute tag*
this morning	*heute morgen*
tonight	*heute abend*
where is...?	*wo ist...*
yes	*ja*

Days

Monday	*Montag*
Tuesday	*Dienstag*
Wednesday	*Mittwoch*
Thursday	*Donnerstag*
Friday	*Freitag*
Saturday	*Samstag*
Sunday	*Sonntag*

Numbers

one	*ein*
two	*zwei*
three	*drei*
four	*vier*
five	*fünf*
six	*sechs*
seven	*sieben*
eight	*acht*
nine	*neun*
ten	*zehn*
eleven	*elf*
twelve	*zwölf*
thirteen	*dreizehn*
fourteen	*vierzehn*
fifteen	*fünfzehn*
sixteen	*sechzehn*

twenty	*zwanzig*
thirty	*dreissig*

French
Travel
airport	*l'aéroport*
bus	*un bus*
railway station	*la gare*
taxi	*taxi*
ticket	*un billet*

When you get there
bathroom	*salle de bain*
beer	*biéres*
chair	*chaise*
credit card	*les cartes de crédir*
elevator	*ascenseur*
hotel	*un hôtel*
how much does it cost?	*combien es-cie?*
key	*la clé*
luggage	*les bagages*
my room	*je suis chambre*
restaurant	*le ristorante*
street	*la rue*
table	*la table*
to bed	*se coucher*
toilet	*les toilettes*
travel agency	*une agence de voyage*
wine	*vin*

Communicating
my name is...	*je m'appelle...*
excuse me please	*excusez-moi*
good evening	*bonsoir*

good morning	*bonjour*
goodbye	*au revoir*
hello	*bonjour*
I would like...	*je voudrais...*
I have a problem	*un probléme*
no	*no*
please	*s'il vous plaît*
please help me	*pouvez-vous n'aider?*
see you later	*a bientôt*
sorry or pardon	*pardon*
thank you (very much)	*merci (beaucoup)*
this afternoon	*ceci aprés-midi*
this morning	*ceci matin*
tonight	*ce soir*
where is...?	*où est...*
yes	*oui*

Days

Monday	*Lundi*
Tuesday	*Mardi*
Wednesday	*Mercredi*
Thursday	*Jeudi*
Friday	*Vendredi*
Saturday	*Samedi*
Sunday	*Dimanche*

Numbers

one	*un*
two	*deux*
three	*trois*
four	*quartre*
five	*cinq*
six	*six*
seven	*sept*

eight	*huit*
nine	*neuf*
ten	*dix*
eleven	*onze*
twelve	*douze*
thirteen	*treize*
fourteen	*quatorze*
fifteen	*quinze*
sixteen	*seize*
twenty	*vingt*
thirty	*trente*

European Time Zones

A table for comparison, if you are coming in from another European city.

City	Hours from AEST	from GMT	from NY time
Amsterdam	-10	+1	+6
Athens	-9	+2	+7
Barcelona	-10	+1	+6
Berlin	-10	+1	+6
Brussels	-10	+1	+6
Copenhagen	-10	+1	+6
Dublin	-11	+0	+7
Frankfurt	-10	+1	+6
Lisbon	-11	0	+7
London	-11	0	+5
Madrid	-10	+1	+6
Manchester	-11	0	+5
Paris	-10	+1	+6
Rome	-10	+1	+6
Venice	-10	+1	+6
Vienna	-10	+1	+6
Zurich	-10	+1	+6

Clothing Sizes And Conversion Chart

Women's Clothing
Coats, Skirts, Dresses, Slacks, Jerseys, Pullovers

Aust/NZ	8	10	12	14	16	18
Europe	38	40	42	44	46	48
UK	8	10	12	14	16	18
USA	6	8	10	12	14	16

Shoes

Aust/NZ	4	5	$5^{1/2}$	6	$6^{1/2}$	7	$7^{1/2}$	8	$8^{1/2}$	9	$9^{1/2}$ 10
Europe	34	36	37	37	38	38	39	40	40	41	41 -
UK	3	$3^{1/2}$	4	$4^{1/2}$	5	$5^{1/2}$	6	$6^{1/2}$	7	$7^{1/2}$	8 $8^{1/2}$
USA	$4^{1/2}$	5	$5^{1/2}$	6	$6^{1/2}$	7	$7^{1/2}$	8	$8^{1/2}$	9	$9^{1/2}$ 10

Men's Clothing
Suits, Coats, Trousers, Jerseys, Pullovers

Aust/NZ	14	16	18	20	22	24
Europe	46	48	50	52	54	56
UK	36	38	40	42	44	46
USA	36	38	40	42	44	46

Shirts (Collar Sizes)

Aust/NZ	15	$15^{1/2}$	16	$16^{1/2}$	17	$17^{1/2}$
Europe (cm)	38	39	41	42	43	44
UK	15	$15^{1/2}$	16	$16^{1/2}$	17	$17^{1/2}$
USA	15	$15^{1/2}$	16	$16^{1/2}$	17	$17^{1/2}$

Shoes

Aust/NZ	8	9	10	11	12	13
Europe	42	43	44	46	47	48
UK	8	9	10	11	12	13
USA	$8^{1/2}$	$9^{1/2}$	$10^{1/2}$	$11^{1/2}$	$12^{1/2}$	$13^{1/2}$

Cameras and Film

For travellers to Germany, Austria and Switzerland it is normally far cheaper to buy the film at your favourite camera shop duty free and have all the films processed when you return home. X-ray security machines in airports can damage photo film when it travels through them, if the film is exposed to this treatment too often on your trip. Better to keep the film roll tucked safely away in its little cylinder. One suggestion is to put all your film in a plastic bag and have it passed through the security check outside the machine.

Be sure to take spare batteries, since the duration of your trip and the fact that you can't remember when you last replaced them may mean a camera dies on you at the most inappropriate sightseeing time.

Mail and Contacting Home

The best way these days to let everyone at home now how your trip is progressing is to get an email address on a free email service such as Yahoo or Hotmail. Teach those in your family who don't know how to access emails before you leave. Addresses can be accessed in any cyber cafe - and there are plenty in Germany, Austria and Switzerland. Or you may be staying with family or friends who are hooked up to the web.

Phone cards are an alternative that allow you to cap the cost of your calls and control your expenditures. VISA has a system which utilises access through a phone company and all you need is to find a public phone.

You can send mail care of an American Express office as long as the recipient has an AMEX card. You should check if they accept parcels. American Express offices will hold the mail for 30 days and this service is free. For most post offices the service is free also, though there may be a holding fee of a couple of dollars in some countries. If you are sending material or having it sent make sure the sender puts a return address on the letter or parcel.

Post offices also have the same system the world over. Just include as much information as possible on the parcel/package/postcard that your are sending.

Keeping Up-To-Date

Please note that because some places close and others open quite frequently, we would greatly appreciate hearing about it. Travel information must always be updated, developed and improved, so if over time any facts in this book have become incorrect, please let us know to help make your next Short Stay Guide accurate.

Have a great trip. We hope our guide enhances your Germany, Austria and Switzerland experience.

Opernplatz, looking towards
Reuterweg, Frankfurt

PART TWO

Germany

THE FEDERAL REPUBLIC OF GERMANY is situated in central Europe and has an area of 356,910 sq km. The population is around 82,000,000 and the official language is German. English is taught in schools, and most people in the hospitality industry are fluent in English.

Climate

The climate is generally mild, with harsher winters in the Bavarian Alps. The July average is 21C, and the January average -1C.

Entry Regulations

Visitors must have a valid passport, and a visa is not required for visits of up to three months.

The duty free allowance is 200 cigarettes, 100 cigarillos or 50 cigars or 250 gm of tobacco; 1 litre of spirits (more than 22 degrees proof) or 2 litres of spirits (up to 22 degrees proof) and 2 litres of sparkling wine and 2 litres of still wine, or a proportional assortment of these products; and 50 grammes of perfume. There is no restriction on the import or export of local or foreign currencies.

No vaccinations are required for any international traveller.

Currency

The Euro will be introduced in January 2002. The previous currency of the land was the Deutsche Mark (DM), which is divided into 100 Pfennigs. Prices in this book pre-date the official change-over, and so are given in DM. Use the table below to convert prices to the new currency after it is put in place.

Approximate exchange rates, which should be used as a guide only, are:

1 Euro = 1.95583 DM
A$ = 1.11DM
Can$ = 1.37DM
NZ$ = 0.90DM
S$ = 1.18DM
UK£ = 3.15DM
US$ = 2.17DM

Banks are ☼open Mon-Fri 9am-noon, 2-4pm. The Reisebanks at Zoo Station and Ostbahnhof are ☼open daily from 7.30am.

Shopping hours are ☼Mon-Fri 9am-6.30pm (Thurs until 8.30pm), Sat 9am-2pm (until 4pm on the first Sat of each month). Shops are closed on Sundays. The big stores in Berlin are ☼open Mon-Fri 9am-8pm, Sat 9am-4pm.

Post Offices are ☼open Mon-Fri 8am-6pm, Sat 8am-noon.

Credit cards are widely accepted.

Telephone

International direct dialling is available and the International code is 00, the country code 49. International calls can be made from booths marked 'Auslandsgesprache', or from post offices.

Payphones have slots for 10 Pfennigs, 1DM and 5DM, or phonecards (Telefonkarten) are available at post offices. Booths where these can be used are marked 'Kartentelefon'. Reverse charge (collect) calls can only be made to the United States.

It is very expensive to make international calls from hotels.

Driving

Germany has nearly 11,000km of toll-free motorways (autobahn), as well as highways that are famous worldwide for their scenic countryside.

UK, American and Canadian citizens can hire a car with a valid driving licence from their own country, other nationalities require an international driver's licence. Traffic drives on the right, seat belts are compulsory, and children under 12 years are not permitted to travel in the front seat.

Speed limits are:

> Built-up areas - 50kph
> Open roads - 100kph
> Motorways - 130kph

Miscellaneous

Local time is GMT + 1, and there is daylight saving in the summer time.

Electricity - 220v AC 50 Hertz, with round ended two-pin plugs.

Health - Visitors from EC countries are covered for medical costs, but all other travellers should have health insurance.

Berlin

Berlin lies in the north German lowlands, on the banks of the Spree River, and its name comes from a Slovakian word meaning 'built on a marsh'. The city has an area of 892 sq km, and it is the third largest in Europe (only London and Paris are larger). It measures 45km from east to west and 38km from north to south, and is divided into 23 districts, each one a city in itself. The population is around 3.5 million.

Although the Wall came down in 1990, Berliners still think of themselves as either Ossis (East) or Wessis (West), as a large proportion cannot remember life before the Wall.

History

History first records Berlin as a city in 1251, in competition with the city of Colln, on the left bank of the Spree. The two cities combined in 1307, under the name of Berlin.

Berlin has had a colourful history ever since the elector of Brandenburg made it his official residence in 1447. It was involved in the Thirty Years War that began in 1618, was invaded by Napoleon in 1806, warred with Austria in 1866, and France in 1870, and was made the capital city of the German Empire in 1871. In 1914, the First World War commenced when Germany invaded France, and in 1918 it concluded with Germany's defeat. Kaiser Wilhelm II abdicated, and the Weimar Republic was established in the same year.

1933 saw Hitler elected, and under his leadership Germany headed for the Second World War, invading Poland in 1939. Once again Germany was defeated, and in 1945 the Allied armies entered Berlin and divided it into four sectors.

The communist DDR (German Democratic Republic) built the Wall in 1961, dividing Berlin into East and West. After the demolition of the wall, all-German elections were held in 1990 and the Christian Democrat coalition was voted into power. Berlin once again became the seat of parliament in 1991.

Tourist Information

The Berlin Tourist Office has several branches: on the ground floor of the Europa Center, Budapester Strasse entrance, ☉open Mon-Sat 8.30am-8.30pm, Sun 10am-6.30pm, ✆(030) 250 025; Tegel Airport Main Hall, ☉open daily 5am-10.30pm; KaDeWe, Travel Centre, ground floor, ☉open Mon-Fri 9.30am-8pm, Sat 9am-4pm.; Brandenburg Gate, South Wing, ☉open daily 9.30am-6pm.

The Berlin Information Centre, Hardenbergstrasse 20, 1000 Berlin 12, has plenty of free maps and brochures.

Local Transport

Public transport in Berlin consists of the U-Bahn (underground), S-Bahn trains, single and double-decker buses. The East is serviced by trams.

Unfortunately, using the **underground system** in the city is confusing and time consuming, with several transfers often necessary to get from A to B. Many U-Bahn stations are inundated with signs that only add to the confusion, as they tell of transfers, exits, transit directions, but there is a shortage of signs telling travellers where they are. Also, there are few stations that have local maps to aid orientation.

Electric **trams** were invented in Berlin, with the first one going into service in 1881. The trams in East Berlin have rattley old carriages, but those in Potsdam are in good repair. Tram stops have HH signs.

Buses can be just as confusing as the underground, but if you enjoy the double-decker variety, why not try to come to grips with the system. **Remember the front stairs are for going up, the back for going down**. Bus stops have a green H on them.

There are different kinds of reduced fare tickets available from ticket offices or, more conveniently, from machines. It may pay you to invest in a *WelcomeCard* book of vouchers for ✪DM29. It offers three days travelling around Berlin and Potsdam on all buses and train operating within the A, B and C fare zones of Berlin, plus discounts of up to 50% for entry to many attractions. The Card is a bonus for families because it entitles every adult to take up to three children under the age of 14 for free. The Cards are available from all BVG ticket offices, tourist information points and some hotels.

A tip for finding your way around Berlin: street numbers run up one side of a street, then down the other, so that no. 2 may be opposite no. 300, depending on the length of the street. The street numbers for each block are indicated on signs on street corners.

Accommodation

As mentioned previously, Berlin is a big city, so you can expect to find plenty of accommodation. Following are a few of the inner city accommodation outlets, with prices in DM that should be used as a guide only. The telephone area code is 030.

Alsterhof Ringhotel Berlin, Augsburger Strasse 5, ✆212 420, fax 218 3949. 200 rooms, a restaurant, bar/lounge and swimming pool - ✪225-390DM including buffet breakfast.

> *Hotel Am Zoo*
>
> Kürfurstendamm 25, ✆884 370, fax 8843 7714. There are 136 rooms, some of which have good views overlooking the Kurfürstendamm. Trendy bar and an adequate dining area - ✪328-485DM including buffet breakfast.

Hotel Avantgarde, Kurfurstendamm 15, 10719 Berlin, ✆882 6466, fax 882 4011. 27 rooms and a combined bar and lounge - ✪230-380DM, including breakfast.

Best Western Hotel Boulevard, Kurfurstendamm 12, ✆884 250, fax 8842 5450. 114 beds and a bar - ✪204-320DM, including buffet breakfast.

Berlin Plaza Hotel, Knesebeckstrasse 63, ✆884 130, fax 9941 3754. 221 beds with facilities including a restaurant and bar - ✪199-339DM including buffet breakfast.

Hotel Berliner Hof, Tauentzienstrasse 8, ✆254 950 fax 262 3065. 80 beds - ✪240-280DM including buffet breakfast.

Food and Drink

Traditional Berlin fare, such as blockwurst and meat balls, is in small supply, but there are still a few places that stick with the originals. Here is a selection.

Wilhelm Hoeck, Charlottenburg, Wilmersdorfer Strasse 149, ✆341 8174 - ◌open Mon-Sat 8am-midnight. Home made meat rissoles, gherkins and pickled eggs near the draught beer taps. This is as Old Berlin as you can get.

Laternchen, Charlottenburg, Windscheidstrasse 24, ✆324 6882 - ◌open Mon-Fri 6pm-midnight, Sat-Sun 6pm-1am. The decor is definitely Old Berlin, but sometimes the menu can have a few imports.

Marjellchen, Charlottenburg, Mommsenstrasse 9, ✆883 2676 - ◌open Mon-Sat noon-midnight, Sun 5pm-midnight. Believed by some to have the best Konigsberg dumplings in town, this eatery also has alcoholic Danzig Goldwasser on offer.

Zur letzten Instanz, Mitte, Waisenstrasse 14-16, ✆242 5528 - ◌open daily noon-1am. This is one of, if not the oldest pub in Berlin, dating back to 1621. In keeping with this reputation there is always "Eisbein" (pickled pork shank) on the menu.

Germans are prolific beer-drinkers, so it is not difficult to locate a pub, in fact there seems to be one on every corner.

Shopping

The best known department store in Berlin is the Kaufhaus des Westens, better known as **KaDeWe**, in Wittenbergplatz. It opened in 1907, and is the largest department store in Germany, and the third largest in Europe - Galeries Lafayette in Paris is the largest, followed by Harrods in London.

KaDeWe has seven floors, but it is the sixth floor that almost puts the store in the sightseeing category, for this is where the legendary giant delicatessen is found.

The ***Europa Centre*** at Breitscheidplatz has a shopping centre, and shopping streets are: Kurfurstendamm and its side streets; Schloss Strasse in Steglitz; Wilmersdorfer Strasse in Charlottenburg; Savignyplatz; Savignybogen; and Under den Linden between Brandenburger Tor and Alexanderplatz.

Forms for reclaiming VAT are issued with the purchase, and the refund is issued when leaving Germany.

Sightseeing

Charlottenburg

The centre of unified Berlin is in the district of Charlottenburg, and this is the best place to begin a tour.

The **Kaiser-Wilhelm-Gedachtniskirche** (Emperor William Memorial Church) on Breitscheidplatz, ✆245 023, was almost completely destroyed during World War II, due to its proximity to the strategically important Zoo station. The powers that be wanted to raze the ruins, but Berlin magazines aroused public interest in the project and a new complex has risen from the ashes. Guided tours are available on ☉Thurs and Fri at 1.15pm, 3pm and 4.30pm, and it is worth visiting for the beautiful mosaic ceiling in the small hall. This is as beautiful as the original church, which is not what some think about the rest of the building.

Kurfurstendamm, affectionately called Ku'damm, branches off opposite the church. This street is 3.5km long and 60m wide, and Otto von Bismarck, the first German chancellor, decided to make it into a shopping and amusement avenue. Apparently he had become enamoured of the Champs Elysees during a trip to Paris in 1871, and wanted to make the Ku'damm as famous, if not more so. All buildings were to be four storeys, and the facades had to be decorated with stucco. English gardens were to be laid out in the front of the houses, and those on the corners had to have a dome on top. It was magnificent but, unfortunately, World War II destroyed 202 of the original 250 buildings.

Fasanenstrasse runs off Ku'damm, and at no. 79-80 is the **Judisches Gemeindehaus** (Jewish Community House), ✆883 6548. This modern centre for Berlin's 6000 Jews was built on the foundations of a Byzantine synagogue that was burned to the ground on infamous Kristallnacht, November 9, 1938. The present building has fragments of the former portal in the entrance. A bronze sculpture by Richard Hess stands in front of the building and has an inscription from the book of Moses.

Back on Breitscheidplatz is the **Europa Centre**, the building with the Mercedes symbol on the top. This twenty-three storey building has more than one hundred shops and restaurants, a casino, *La Vie en Rose* nightclub, the Tourist Office and various airline offices. A **Panoramic Lookout** is a few steps up from the 22nd floor, and access is on Tauentzienstrasse between the Dresdner Bank and the cinema. This tower is ◌open daily 9am-midnight, and admission is ✪DM5, but it is worth it on a clear day.

The Europa Centre stands where the famous Romanische Cafe stood before it was destroyed in the war.

Opposite the Europa Centre and the Memorial Church is the **State Art Gallery**, which is sometimes used for exhibitions.

The **Bahnhof Zoo** (Zoo Train Station) was completely renovated for the 750th anniversary of Berlin in 1987. It is both a mainline and S-Bahn station as well as a U-Bahn station in the annex. The station has an information counter, a hotel reservation display, a bookstore and lockers, and because it is in the middle of the zoo complex, every other kind of shop is in close vicinity.

The **Zoologistche Garten** (Zoo) is across from the station in Hardenbergplatz, ✆2540 1255, and it is ◌open daily 9am-6.30pm (winter 5pm). Home to 11,000 animals, this zoo claims to have more species than any other. Admission is ✪DM10. When Berlin was a divided city a second zoo was established in Friedrichsfelde, the **Tierpark**. It is not as large as the West Berlin establishment, but it does have the largest polar bear collection in the world.

While at the zoo, in West Berlin, you might consider visiting the **Aquarium** which is in the building next to the Elephant Gate. Admission is ✪DM8, or you can get a combined zoo/aquarium ticket for ✪DM12.

From the Zoo underground station take a train to either Sophie-Charlotte Platz, or the more convenient Richard-Wagner Platz, then follow the signs to the Charlottenburg Palace (Schloss), the most beautiful baroque building in Berlin.

Charlottenburg Palace was originally built as an eleven window summer house for Sophie Charlotte, the wife of the future King Friedrich I. It was completed in its present form, with the cream-coloured facade measuring 505m, in 1790.

The palace was severely damaged during the bombing raids of World War II, but there has been much careful restoration. The gardens were originally in the French style, but in the early 19th century they were remodelled into a somewhat disorganised English style. The most recent restoration has preserved the best of both. Interesting buildings in the park include the **Schinkel Pavilion**, a Neapolitan style villa built by Friedrich Wilhelm III and his second wife Princess Liegnitz. It is ⊕open Tues-Sun 10am-5pm. Near the banks of the Spree, at the north of the park is the **Belvedere**, built in 1788 as a teahouse for Friedrich Wilhelm II. It is ⊕open Tues-Sun 10am-5pm.

At the end of a line of fir trees on the west side of the park is the **Mausoleum**, ⊕open Tues-Sun 10am-5pm. This temple was built by Friedrich Wilhelm III for his Queen Liuse. Several other royals have been interred here.

The **Historical Rooms** (Historische Raume) of the Palace are ⊙open to the general public Tues-Sun 10am-5pm, Thurs until 8pm, and admission for all buildings and rooms is ✪8DM. This is another opportunity to see how royalty spent their waking and sleeping moments, but don't expect this tour to be another Versailles.

The **Orangerie** at the west end of the palace was built as a hothouse, became a theatre during the late 1780s, and is now a coffee shop.

Museums

Whilst in this area there are a few museums to visit. The **Egyptian Museum**, 70 Schloss Strasse, ✆320 911, was built as barracks for the royal bodyguards. It now has one of the best Egyptian collections in the world, with two really outstanding pieces - a 3400-year-old bust of the beautiful Nefertiti, wife of Pharaoh Akhenaton, from the Tel el-Amarna period; and the Kalabasha Monumental Gate built around 20BC for the Roman Emperor Augustus. The latter was presented to the museum by the Egyptian government when its site was flooded by the Aswan High Dam; the former was unearthed by a team of German archaeologists in 1912, and, like so many of Egypt's treasures, was "souvenired".

Across from this building is the **Antikenmuseum**, ✆320 911, with a good collection of ancient Greek, Etruscan and Roman art, and the Treasury in the basement has a silver and gold collection dating from around 2000BC.

The **Brohan Museum** is opposite the Palace, ✆321 4029, and is ⊙open Tues-Sun 10am-6pm, Thurs till 8pm. It has a large collection of Art Deco paintings, sculptures, arts and crafts and furniture, collected between 1889 and 1939.

In Sophie-Charlotte Strasse, no. 17-18 is the **Plaster Cast House**, ✆321 7011, ⊙open Mon-Fri 9am-4pm, Wed till 6pm. A bit different from ordinary museums, this is a branch of the Prussian Cultural

Foundation, and visitors can buy plaster casts of about 7000 of the foundation's exhibits (even including Nefertiti).

Heading away from Charlottenburg, travel along Otto-Suhr Allee to Ernst Reuter Platz, named for the first mayor of Berlin after the Second World War, then on to Strasse des 17 Juni, which bisects the **Technical University**. Follow this street to the **Charlottenburger Tor**, over the Landwehr Canal. This was the entrance to Charlottenburg from the Tiergarten district, and was built in 1905, the 200th anniversary of the death of Sophie Charlotte. On the left of the gate is Friedrich I (originally Elector Friedrich III), and on the right is his wife Sophie Charlotte, pointing the way to the Palace. The original gate was larger than at present because in 1937, the size of the columns was reduced to enable Hitler's architect Speer to have enough room for his grand avenue for Nazi victory parades - Charlottenburger Chaussee. The present name of the street is derived from the workers' uprising in East Berlin on June 17, 1953.

Brandenburger Tor

Probably the best way to get to the gate from Charlottenburger is to catch double-decker Bus 100, which begins its journey in front of *McDonald's* at the Zoo train station. Although this is a normal part of the local transport system, it has become popular with sightseers as its route takes in all the important attractions between east and west.

The first stop is the **Europa Center**, then the bus makes its way to Spreeweg, and the stop marked **Grosser Stern** (Big Star). This large roundabout has a **Victory Monument** which can be climbed for a good view of the surrounding area. The bus then continues past Schloss Bellevue, along John Foster Dulles Allee, for a stop in front of the **Kongresshalle** (locally called the Pregnant Oyster, for obvious reasons). The next stop is the Reichstag, then Reichstag Sud (south) in front of the Gate, then past what was the Wall, then a left turn onto **Unter den Linden** (under the lime trees), probably the best-known street in Berlin.

The first **Brandenburg Gate** was part of the walls of the old city, and it was demolished in 1788. The present gate was opened on August 6, 1791, and it is 65.5m wide, 11m thick and 26m high. The central opening is 5.5m and was originally reserved for the use of royal coaches. The 6m quadriga, drawn by four horses, was built in 1794. Originally the winged charioteer was the Greek goddess of peace, Irene. In October 1806, Napoleon took the complete quadriga to Paris, and when it was returned in 1814, the driver had become Victoria, the victory goddess, and she had a laurel wreath and an iron cross. The quadriga was destroyed in World War II, and the East Berlin magistrate had a replica erected in 1958.

Another interesting building in this area is the **Reichstag**, built between 1884 and 1894 as the seat of the German parliament. During World War II it was almost completely ruined, and it stayed that way until the 1960s when the West German parliament decided to rebuild it as a symbol of the desire to reunite the country. There are guided tours ☉daily at 2pm, and an audio tour.

Outside Berlin

Potsdam

The city of Potsdam is south-west of Berlin, and begins across the Glienicke Bridge.

It is the capital city of the state of Brandenburg, and home to a world-famous tourist attraction, the **Sanssouci Palace**.

Built between 1745 and 1747 for the Prussian King Friedrich II, nicknamed 'the Great', the then twelve room castle was used as a summer residence. Friedrich liked to model himself on Louis XIV, the Sun King, so French was often spoken in his court, and one of his courtiers suggested the name 'Sans souci' (French for 'without care') for his new palace.

In 1763-64, after the seven-year war, King Friedrich oversaw the building of the Neues Palais, the Picture Gallery, the New Chambers and the Chinese Teahouse, gathering a lot of his ideas from the Palace of Versailles.

Between 1851 and 1861, Friedrich Wilhelm IV decided to extend the complex, and he was influenced by anything Italian, so his buildings - the Great Orangerie, Charlottenhof Palace and the Roman Baths - reflect this different style.

Whether or not it compares with Versailles is up to each visitor to decide, and unfortunately, entry is not always guaranteed, as curators fear the damage that crowds can inflict on the buildings. As tour groups are given priority, the best thing independent travellers can do is to arrive early, pick up a numbered card, tour the gardens, then return in the afternoon to tour the palace complex.

The opening times (which may change, so check with the information offices) are:

Sanssouci Castle, New Chambers, New Palace, Chinese Tea House, Charlottenhof Castle, Roman Baths:

- February-September - 9am-5pm
- October - 9am-4pm
- November-January - 9am-3pm (Lunch break 12.30pm-1pm)
- Closed every 1st and 3rd Monday of the month.

Ladies' Wing and Orangerie Castle:

- Middle of May to the middle of October only.

Admission is from ✪5DM (Ladies' Wing) to 10DM (Sanssouci).

Note that some parts may only be visited with a guide.

To get there by car: Autobahn Berliner Ring, Bundes-strasse 1 or 273.

By train: Regional train R3 to Potsdam Kaiserbahnhof. S-Bahn from Berlin to Potsdam Stadt, then by tram to Luisenplatz, or the Bus line A to Sanssouci.

For further information contact Potsdam Information, Friedrich Ebert Strasse 5 D-14467 Potsdam, ℂ(0331) 275 580, fax 275 5899 (www.potsdam.de).

The Best of Berlin in Brief

Egyptian Museum (Ägyptisches Museum). The jewel of this treasure-packed museum is seeing the bust that depicts the ancient Queen Nefertiti. *Schloss-strasse 70*.

Charlottenburg Palace (Schloss Charlottenburg). This baroque palace used to be a residence of Prussian royalty. Some works from the baroque period which were collected by the royals are on display in the publicly-accessible rooms. *Luisenplatz*.

The Museum of the Wall (Museum Haus am Checkpoint Charlie). Traces the history of the Berlin Wall from its sudden construction to its heady demise, detailing escapes, both successful and failed, and outlining the pervading consequences its existence had on the city. *Friedrichstrasse 44*.

Tiergarten. This landscaped public park occupies a large portion of central Berlin. In its midst is the giant Victory Column (Siegessaule), from the top of which you can take in a panoramic view of Berlin.

Berlin Zoo (Zoologischer Garten Berlin). Located in Tiergarten, the Berlin Zoo houses a wide array of animals. The pandas are the most popular exhibit.

Gemaldegalerie. Fine German, Italian and Dutch paintings, from the talented hands of Rembrandt, Bruegel, Bosch, Bottiecelli, Raphael and others. Over 600 works are on display in this celebrated gallery. *Mattaiskirchplatz 4.*

Kurfurstendamm. A shopping district with up-market boutiques and trendy cafes serving coffee to keep you on your feet.

Kaiser Wilhelm Memorial Church (Gedachtniskirche). This church is still in ruins after its bombing during WWII, and has an interesting exhibit of the event. *Kurfurstendamm.*

Kaufhaus des Westens ("KaDeWe"). A massive department storing selling everything including the kitchen sink - a staggering variety of merchandise, and a noteworthy food section. *Wittenbergplatz.*

Natural History Museum (Museum fur Naturkunde). The highlight is the huge complete dinosaur skeleton, the world's largest.

German Cathedral. Contains an interesting history of Germany.

Deutsche Guggenheim Berlin. Contemporary modern art with an emphasis on encouraging young artisits. There are also works from better-known people like Cezanne. *Unter den Linden 13-15.*

Pergamon Museum. The focus here is on ancient enxhibits, and the most coveted piece is the enormous Pergamon altar, more than 2100 years old, which depicts figures from Greek mythology. *Kupfergraben, Museumsinsel.*

Bonn

In the days of The Wall and a divided country, Bonn was the capital of West Germany and the seat of government. Now it is no longer a centre of power, and has reverted to being simply the birthplace of Beethoven.

Bonn sits on the west bank of the Rhine River, approximately 30km south of Cologne.

History

Called Castra Bonnensia by the Romans when they had a full-strength legionary post on the site, Bonn was the residence of the Prince-Bishops of Cologne for about five hundred years.

During the Napoleonic era the city was occupied by his armies, and after his defeat it became part of Prussia in 1815. Shortly after this the University came into being.

Before the Second World War, Bonn was a quiet, attractive university town, but during the war the town centre was heavily bombed and suffered almost complete destruction. In 1949 Bonn was made the seat of the Federal Government, which caused its population to double. The town has been almost completely restored in the post war period.

Tourist Information

The Tourist Information Centre, Cassius-passage, Munsterstrasse 20, 53103 Bonn, ✆(0228) 773 466, is ⊙open Mon-Fri 9am-6.30pm, Sat 9am-5pm, Sun and public holidays 10am-2pm. (✇www.bonn-regio.de)

There is a branch of the German National Tourist Office at Niebuhrstrasse 16b, ✆(0228) 214 071-72.

Sightseeing

Most of the old town is a pedestrian zone enclosed by a ring road, and the centre is the **Marktplatz**, a triangular-shaped area that has on one corner the 18th century **Town Hall**. An annex of the town hall can be entered from Rathausgasse, and it contains the city's **art collection**.

From the western corner of Marktplatz, Bonn-gasee branches off, and at no. 20 is the **Beethovenhaus** where the great composer was born in 1770. The house is now a museum dedicated to Beethoven and has been completely restored. It is ☉open Mon-Sat 10am-5pm, Sun 10am-1pm.

South-west of the Marktplatz is the **Munster St Martin**, in Munsterplatz. A Romanesque style basilica of the 12th-13th century, the church is worth visiting for its original wall paintings. Take Remisius-strasse which runs off Munsterplatz, then turn right into Furstenstrasse and continue to Am Hof, part of the ring road. Opposite are the main buildings of the **Friedrich Wilhelms Universitat**, the university of Bonn. These buildings formed the residential palace of the Prince-Electors of Cologne.

South-west of the Munster is the main railway station, and not far from there, at 14-16 Colmantstrasse, is the **Rheinisches Landesmuseum**. It has a good collection of sculptures, paintings and antiquities, and is ☉open Tues, Thurs 9am-5pm, Wed 9am-8pm, Fri 9am-4pm, Sat-Sun 11am-5pm.

Most of the important government buildings, including the home of the President of the Federal Republic, are in Adenauerallee. It runs parallel to, but not alongside, the Rhine.

Bad Godesberg, about 7km to the south, is a spa resort and home to several diplomatic missions. It can be reached by rail or by the B9 road. The town dates back to Roman times, but its dubious claim to fame is that it was where Adolf Hitler and Neville Chamberlain, the then Prime Minister of Britain, met in 1938 to discuss the fate of Czechoslovakia. While in Bad Godesberg, look out for Godesburg, a ruined 13th century castle that has been restored as a hotel.

The Best of Bonn in Brief

Beethoven's House. A museum has been established inside the famous composer's birthplace.

Town Hall. A good example of the Rococo style.

The Royal Palace. Created late in the baroque period.

Bonn's Museums. Visit the German History Museum (Haus der Geschichte), the Art and Exhibition Hall (Kunstund Ausstellungshalle), the Art Museum (Kunstmuseum Bonn), and the Alexander Koenig Museum, all of which are in close proximity to each other.

Cologne

Cologne (Köln) is situated on the left bank of the Rhine, 40km south of Dusseldorf, and is over 2000 years old. Cologne was badly damaged during World War II, but most of the very old buildings have been carefully restored.

Many people visit Cologne during Fastelovend (Carnival) which begins on New Year's Eve and continues until the Monday before Ash Wednesday! Originally held to celebrate the end of winter it is now more of a time to let your hair down, with more than 300 balls held during the festival. It climaxes with a procession on Rosenmontag (Rose Monday).

The Cathedral - the famous Dom - that in part was the only thing standing after the Second World War - is the centre of town. Not far away is the famous address of 4711 (Eau de Cologne).

In many ways this city is off the beaten track as far as international visitors are concerned. Most people go to Cologne by rail or car, though there is an international airport nearby. Bonn, the former capital, is just down the road, so to speak.

History

Cologne was founded by the Romans in 38BC, and many remains from this period are still in situ. The cultural and commercial capital of the Rhineland, Cologne was guaranteed an important part in world affairs, because of its strategic position where the trade routes from the four compass points met. Today it is well known world-wide for its trade fairs, something of a carryover from the markets of earlier times.

Tourist Information

There is a very helpful information office opposite the cathedral at Untere Fettenhenen 19, D-50667, Köln, ✆(0221) 221 23345, fax 221 23320. (👁www.koeln.org/koelntourismus, email ✎koelntourismus@stadt-koeln.de). Their 🕐opening hours are:

Winter (1 November to April 30th) 8.00am-9.00pm Monday to Saturday, Sunday and Public Holidays 9.30am-7.00pm.

Summer (1 May to 31 October) 8.00am-10.30pm Monday to Saturday, Sunday and Public Holidays 9.00am-10.30pm

Local Transport

The widely spread network of U-Bahn (underground), trams and buses that connect with the S-Bahn (city train) traffic of the Ruhr network, gives optimal public transport coverage.

Accommodation

Here the prices are for a double with an ensuite. Credit cards are accepted, and both heating and air-conditioning are part of the package. When booking a hotel room in Germany, especially on the web, browse the range of the booking agencies that come up when you conduct your search. Check out the prices and go for the cheapest as they are not always the same and you can always get a deal.

Note that on the day you arrive you can also book at the Tourist Information office for accommodation that night.

Ambassador Hotel, Barbarossaplatz 4a, ⓒ49-211 568 900 for bookings. 50 rooms, family run, restaurant, rooms are relatively large - ✪240DM.

Antik Hotel Bristol

Kaiser-Willhelm Ring 48, ⓒ49-221 12 0195, fax 221-13 1495. 44 rooms, city centre. A private hotel that affords a very pleasant stay in quality surroundings. The decor is replete with antiques and the friendly service makes this a very nice hotel. Restaurant, bar, parking, concierge, currency exchange - ✪230DM.

Sofitel Mondial Am Dom, Kurt Hackenberg Platz 1, 50667 Cologne, ⓒ49-221 2 0630, fax 221 206 3522, email ✎H1306@accor-hotels.com. 205 rooms, Pacific Bar, Beer Pub Prost, 2 restaurants. Opposite Cathedral, Ludwig Museum and Philharmonic Hall - ✪250DM.

Mercure Severinshof is a first class hotel in the downtown area. Facilities include restautant, bar and health club.

There are three **Youth Hostels** in Cologne:
Deutz, Siegesstrasse 5a, ⓒ(221) 814 711, fax (221) 884 425.

Riehl Jugendgastehaus, An der Schanz 14, ✆(221) 767 081, fax (221) 761 555.
Station-Backpacker's Hostel, Marzellenstrasse 44-48, ✆(221) 912 5301, fax 912 5303.

Food and Drink

Surprisingly, because Cologne is set on a river famous for its wines, the city has some of the best local beer in Germany, called *Kolsch* (which means 'belonging to Köln').

There is no special dish that is associated with Cologne, but you can be guaranteed a hearty meal in any establishment serving local food, rather than international.

Sightseeing

The obvious place to begin a tour is the **Cathedral** (Dom). Work on the building began in 1248, but it was not completed until 1842. Fortunately, though, no one lost the plans because the Gothic style was carried through to the end. During World War II, 90 per cent of the old town area was destroyed, but the Cathedral, though sustaining much damage, was still standing.

The inside of the church is very peaceful, even though it is in the middle of the hustle and bustle of the city. There is a viewing platform 97m above the city in the south tower, but there are 509 steps to be dealt with to get there. Many works of art are to be found inside, among them a wooden crucifix carved in 969, the Bible window in the choir, the Shrine of the Magi (pictured) which is said to hold relics of the Three Kings, a mosaic floor in the choir. The cathedral treasury is also worth a visit.

The main railway station (hauptbahnhoff) of the city is centred next to the Dom. This area is the transport hub of the city.

The square building on the left, facing the cathedral's east end, is the **Romisch-Germanisches Museum**, which was built over the Roman Dionysus Mosaic. The mosaic was found when workmen were excavating to build an air-raid shelter during the Second World War. The museum has many other exhibits of life in Cologne from Roman times to the reign of Charlemagne.

Along Unter Goldschmied strasse is a 100m long Roman drainage channel that you can walk along (the new Town Hall is also here), and the remains of the **Roman town wall** around the corner of Komodien and Tunis strasses and the corner of Zeughaus and Auf dem Berlich strasses. On the left of the new **Town Hall** is the centre of the old town, which is a pedestrian zone, and nearby is **St Martin's Church** which is surrounded by new buildings that blend in with the old (an early example of the present day interest in preserving the past). This part of the old town is the **Alter Markt** (old market) and there are several ale houses and eateries in and around, such as *Papa Joe's Biersalon*, Alter Markt 50-52, where non-traditional New Orleans jazz features, and the *Gaffelhaus* traditional restaurant at Alter Markt 20-22. Then head for Heumarkt (Haymarket), and at no. 60 there is *Altstadt Paffgen*, where you can grab a bite to eat, and maybe try some of the Kolsch beer.

Take Gurzenichstrasse from Heumarkt, then turn right into Unter Goldschmied and you will see the **Gurzenich**, a Gothic festival hall that was completed in 1444, and rebuilt after the Second World War. From here take Obenmarspforte to Hohe strasse, a pedestrian mall that leads back towards the cathedral.

Alternatively, stay on Obenmarspforte until you reach the Offenbachplatz, then take special notice of the large Renaissance style building, or more importantly, its street number - **4711**. This is where the chemist who produced the formula for Kölnisch Wasser, or as it is better known, Eau de Cologne, lived. The house is now a perfume museum, and it has an interesting clock that puts on a performance ☺every hour from 9am to 9pm.

The streets in Köln or Cologne, however you want to pronounce it, are fairly wide and graced with many trees. An efficient tram service operates throughout the city, and the local people are most helpful in the main in giving directions.

For attractions further afield, the northern edge of the city has the Zoological Gardens and Aquarium, and in summer an aerial cableway operates across the Rhine from the zoo, offering fantastic views of the city and the cathedral. Next to the zoo is the Botanical Gardens.

The Best of Cologne in Brief

Cathedral. Germany's largest cathedral, 600 years in the making, has many points of interest and should definitely be visited if you are in Köln.

Roman Churches. Twelve picturesque churches erected in the Roman period are to be found in the inner-city area.

Wallraf-Richartz and Ludwig Museums. More art from the famous greats in the Wallraf-Richartz is balanced by the twentieth-century works featured in the neighbouring Ludwig.

Romisch-Germanisches Museum. Wonderful collection of Roman antiquities somewhat diminished by the fact that details of the displays are only recorded in German.

Kölner Philharmonie. A famous concert hall.

Imhoff-Stollwerck Chocolate Museum. Situated on the banks of the Rheine, this modern museum explains the process of chocolate making with a history of the pratice and, of course, a taste of the product.

Town Hall. A treasure from the medieval era.

Rheingarten. Head here for a taste of beer from the local brewers.

Frankfurt am Main

The city of Frankfurt is situated at the crossroads of Germany. It has a population of around 625,000 and is one of the world's great financial centres.

This city possesses the most dynamic and professional event organisers in the world. It has become the hub for many international airlines who bring millions of people to Frankfurt every year to attend a conference, convention or fair - industrial or commercial - held at the famous Messe. The Messe stretches for kilometres with at least 10 convention halls and is some 3 floors high. Mini buses run all day to transport fair-goers from one part of the complex to another.

Most of the old part of the city was destroyed by bombing during the Second World War, so much of what is seen now is not original.

Tourist Information

Information centres are found at: the main railway station, opposite track 23 - ☉open Mon-Fri 8am-9pm, Sat-Sun 9am-6pm, ✆(069) 212 388 00, fax 212 378 80; Romerberg 27 - ☉open Mon-Fri 9.30am-5.30pm, Sat-Sun and public holidays 10am-4pm. (✉tct.frankfurt.de)

Local Transport

Frankfurt has rail, underground, bus and tram services, with the latter being the most efficient way of getting around the city.

Accommodation

Several hundred hotels live off the Messe, as do the countless restaurants, bars and shops in the area.

It is best to book and visit Frankfurt when a fair is not on, especially the Book Fair normally held in October. Every available room is booked out at this time and the prices are not cheap.

Prices are for a double and include the VAT of 10%. The hotels tend to be functional rather than glamorous, and those listed here are around or near the Hauftbanhof - Central Railway station on Baselerstrasse, or nearby streets. Running south from the Railway station you can find yourself very quickly in the Red Light district of the city.

There is a web site that is excellent for information on accommodation in Frankfurt called ✉www.dunia.org/germany/city/hotels. You will have to book your hotel through them, as they give you no information on phone numbers, faxes or actual street address, though each hotel is accompanied with a map to give you some idea of where it is located. Another web address well worth checking on is ✉www.frankfurt-online.net/hotel

Carlton Hotel

Karlstrasse 11, 60329 Frankfurt, ©69-232 093, fax 66306-600. This small, stylish, boutique hotel has 27 rooms on 5 storeys and is located in the middle of the business district. Excellent facilities and family-run service will ensure a pleasant stay, particularly for business travellers. ✪130-300DM.

Hotel Europa, Baseler Strasse, 17, ©69-236 013, fax 236 203. 50 rooms with ensuite, tourist class hotel - ✪150-200DM.

Along Baseler Strasse there are countless tourist class hotels - the *Imperial*, the *Hotel Wiesbaden*, the *Excelsior*, the *Manhattan* - all sorts of name that you can imagine. Accommodation is not the problem but the price may be. Either the Tourist Office at the Hauphtbanhof, Airport or the Messe can find you accommodation. Do not be shy in approaching these centres.

Best Western Imperial Hotel am Palmengarten

Sophienstrasse 40, 60487 Frankfurt, ©069-793 0030, fax 069-793 03888. 150 rooms, restaurant, garage, near a park, rooms have all the necessary modcons - ✪190DM.

Hotel Apollo, Mücheneer Strasse 44, 60329 Frankfurt, ©069-23 1285, fax 069-23 2909. 70 rooms, restaurant. This is a two star hotel that is near the centre of town and it is clean and comfortable. Decent prices - ✪60DM in off season.

Pension Adria, Neuhaub Strasse 21, 60322 Frankfurt, ©069-59 4533, fax 069-55 8284. 13 rooms with garage(extra), ensuites, very simple, no phone - ✪60DM.

Arabella Sheraton Grand Hotel Frankfurt is a first class hotel in the midtown area. Facilities include restaurant, bar, coffee shop, health club, swimming pool and shops -

Dorint Hotel is a first class hotel in the midtown area. Facilities include restaurant, bar, coffee shop, health club and swimming pool.

Frankfurt's **Youth Hostel** is:
Haus der Jugend, Deutscherrnufer 12, ✆(069) 619 058, fax 618 257.

Depending on what time of year the prices vary considerably. Best to buy through a tour operator before departure.

You can organise private accommodation at the Messe which is the main reason why a lot of people from overseas visit Frankfurt during the year.

Accommodation Service - Messe Frankfurt GmbH, fax (069) 7575 6352, Torhaus Service Centre, Level 3.

Telephone for enquiries, not for reservations:
Hotel Accommodation: ✆(069) 7575 6222, ✆7575 6695.
Private Accommodation: ✆7575 6296, ✆7575 6696.

Food and Drink

In the district of Sachsenhausen apple cider is sold at the world famous Apfelweinlokale. This area of Frankfurt is dotted with many restaurants.

Around the Opera House and along the main avenues there are some excellent restaurants. Across the river along Gartenstrasse, and around the Dom (old Cathedral - recently restored) and Town Hall (Romer) there is a delightful selection. Many people gravitate to the ubiquitous McDonald's, and Movenpic are also well represented in Frankfurt.

Sightseeing

Frankfurt's favourite son is Johann Wolfgang von Goethe, the famous author, and he was baptised in **Katharinekirche**, which is opposite the **Hauptwache** (Guard House), a junction for the above ground and underground rail systems. The Guard House was built in 1730, and is a good place to begin a tour of the city.

There are a couple of other churches in this vicinity - the **Liebfrauenkirche** and the **Paulskirche**. St Paul's was built 1789-1833, but was burnt to the ground in 1944. Because of its historical significance as the meeting place of the German National Assembly in the 1840s, people from all over the country donated the money to have it rebuilt.

Not far from St Paul's, at 23 Grosser Hirschgraben, is **Goethehaus**, where the great man was born and lived. It is now a museum, and is ☉open Mon-Sat 9am-6pm, Sun 10am-1pm (April-September); Mon-Sat 9am-4pm, Sun 10am-1pm (October-March).

On the nearby Romerberg is the city's restored landmark - the Romer, the town hall complex of buildings. Of them, the **Kaidersaal** (Imperial Hall) in the Zum Romer is ☉open to the public Mon-Sat 9am-5pm, Sun 10am-4pm. The tourist information office is at Romerberg 27, and they have good free maps of the city.

To the left of the Romer is the **Imperial Cathedral** (Kaiserdom), where the German emperors were elected and crowned. The building is from the 14th-15th centuries, and has many works of art including a life-size stone Calvary scene by Hans Backoffen (1509).

From here head towards the river and the **Historisches Museum**, with a varied collection that includes a model of Frankfurt of 1912 and replicas of the crown jewels of the Holy Roman Empire. The museum is ☉open Tues 10am-5pm, Wed 10am-8pm, Thurs-Sat 10am-5pm, and there is no general admission fee.

Other Museums

On the other side of the river from here are seven museums. The **Museum of Arts and Crafts** (Museum fur Kunsthandwerk) has four sections - Far Eastern, European, Islamic, and Books and Writing. It is ☉open Tues-Sun 10am-5pm, Wed until 8pm, and admission is free.

The **Ethnological Museum** (Museum fur Volkerkunde) has a very large collection from the world over. It is ☉open Tues-Sun 10am-5pm, Wed until 8pm, and admission is free.

The **German Film Museum** (Deutsches Filmmuseum) has a good exhibition of cinematographic history. It is ☉open Tues-Sun 11am-6.30pm and admission is free. In the lower ground floor there is a very good cafe.

The **German Architectural Museum** (Deutsches Architekturmuseum) is the only one of its kind in the world, and is only of interest to people involved, or interest in the profession. It is ☉open Tues-Sun 10am-5pm, Wed until 8pm, and admission is free.

The **Postal Museum** (Bundespostmuseum) is only for people with special interests. It is also ☉open Tues-Sun 11am-5pm, Wed until 8pm. Admission is free.

The **Art Institute** (Stadelsches Kunstinstitut) has a collection of 13th to 20th century art that includes works by Rubens, Durer, Rembrandt and Botticelli. It is the only museum in the group to charge admission. ☉Open Tues-Sun 11am-5pm, Wed until 8pm.

Liebighaus is a sculpture museum with exhibits dating back to 3000BC.

These museums are only a 15 minute walk from the old centre of Town. A footbridge across the Main near the old centre of town brings you to the museum area in no time. On the Museum side there is a very pleasant walk along the river bank.

Places Further Afield

Frankfurt has a very modern **Zoo** that can be reached by the underground. The main entrance on Alfred-Brehm-Platz is ⊙open March 16 to September 30 daily 8am-7pm; October 1 to October 15 daily 8am-6pm; February 16 to March 15 8am-6pm. The entrance on Rhonstrasse is ⊙open daily September 16 to March 15 8am-7pm; March 16 to September 15, 8am-6pm.

The **Palmengarten** is to the north of the city and has entrances on Siesmayerstrasse, Bockenheimer Landstrasse, Palmengartenstrasse, Siesmayerstrasse and Zeppelinallee. It has a large greenhouse that simulates tropical jungle conditions; other greenhouses containing tropical and sub-tropical plants; a children's playground; a train ride; and a restaurant. It is ⊙open daily Jan-Feb 9am-4pm, March 9am-5pm, April-Sept 9am-6pm, Oct 9am-5pm, Nov-Dec 9am-4pm, and there is an admission fee.

The town of **Darmstadt** is south of Frankfurt on the Bundesstrasse 3, and it was home to Hesses' grand dukes until 1918. The town's **Castle** was modelled on Versailles and is worth a visit. In the castle museum is the *Darmstadter Madonna* painted by Hans Holbein in 1526, and the Porcelain Museum has the grand dukes' collection of 18th and 19th century porcelain and earthenware.

Another attraction in the town is the **Mathildenhohe**, an artists' colony started by the last grand duke, Ernst-Ludwig. It has several interesting buildings including the Russian Chapel, built in 1899 as a present from Czar Nicholas II to his wife Alexandra, and the Marriage

Tower, built in 1905. Alternatively, you can go to the university (1386 founded) town of **Heidelberg** for the day by car. Situated on the River Neckar. Recommended.

The Best of Frankfurt in Brief

Imperial Cathedral (Kaiserdom). Ten German emperors and kings were crowned here.

Imperial Hall (Kaisersaal). This is where the royals held their lavish banquets, and its doors are open to the public.

St Paul's Church (Paulskirche). Germany's first democratically-elected parliament operated from here.

Guard House (Hauptwache). Once the outpost of the City Guard and also used as a prison.

Town Hall (Romer complex). Completed in the fifteenth century, this building is still the city's Town Hall.

Goethe House (Goethehaus). The home in which the prolific German poet was born.

Old Opera House (Alte Oper). The centre of the city's cultural sphere.

Historical Garden (Historischer Garten). Excavations among these historical gardens uncovered Roman artifacts dating back to the first century AD.

Commerzbank building. This is Europe's tallest office building at a height of 257.7 metres.

Historical Museum (Historisches Museum). A good collection of various artifacts.

Heidelberg

This amazing university town sits on banks of the river Necker, which is spanned by the Bridge of Worms. Heidelberg is dominated by the incredible ruins of the castle of Ludwig. The castle was destroyed in 1689 by French troops in one of this city's celebrated fights with other principalities. In this case it was against Louis XIV who laid claim by inheritance to this beautiful part of the world.

The town is a delightful place with small cobblestone squares and streets, pubs and eateries, bookshops, students' digs, churches, halls, and an environment that is simply very pleasant for an afternoon amble. Do not forget to take the funicular up to the old destroyed castle of Ludwig, part of which is still useable. The stonework and construction is impressive. There are beautiful gardens and you can walk in the park along pleasantly winding paths. The view of the city from the castle is spectacular.

Heidelberg is less than 2 hours by car from Frankfurt, making it perfect for a day trip or an overnight stay.

History

Heidelberg's fame extends to Martin Luther and the Calvinists who had a number of celebrated stouches here in the sixteenth century. Its rulers came and went, oscillating between the protestant elector Friedrich V, then Maximilian of Bavaria, then Tilly, then Karl Ludwig, until Louis XIV of France claimed it.

Meanwhile the populace wanted some say in administration, so rebellions broke out regularly in the city. It was a place of coming and going for armies, scholars and religious notables.

In the 18th century the city was rebuilt based on its old Gothic layout, but in the new Baroque style. In 1815 the Emperor of Austria, the Tsar and the King of Prussia, signed the Holy Alliance here. It was the site of the German National Assembly in 1848. The university has a reputation for scholarship, and escaped bombing during the Second World War. It has many notable Noble Prize winners, and boasts a student population of 28,000 in a population of 135,000. Perhaps for many Americans especially, the film *The Student Prince* has made it a popular place to visit and stay.

Accommodation

Prices are for a double room. When booking accommodation it is important to ask if the hotel has a lift, central heating, and an ensuite. The places listed below do have these facilities. The following internet address is a good one for finding a place to stay and planning your trip ⊚www.cvb-heidelberg.de

Best Western Rega Hotel Heidelberg, Bergheimer Strass 63, 69115 Heidelberg, ✆062 21 5080, fax 062-2150 8500, ⊚www.rega.bestwestern.de. 236 rooms, garage, restaurant, comfortable but not your average Heidelberg student hangout, central heating - ✪250-270DM.

Achat Hotel, Karlsruher Strasse 130, 69126 Heidelberg, ✆062 21 31 0300, fax 062 21 31 03 33. 80 rooms, restaurant, central heating (rather important in this area). A good location in the old part of town towards the river - ✪165DM.

Classic Inn, Belfortstrasse 3, 69115 Heidelberg, ✆062 21-13 8320, fax 062 21-1 38 3238. 40 beds, telephone. This is a simple hotel which is a 3 minute walk at most to the train station - ✪140-165DM.

Elite, Bunsenstr.15, 69115 Heidelberg, ✆062 21-2 5734, fax 062-21 16 3949. 23 rooms, not far from the university clinic and various govenment offices - ✪100DM.

Munich

Munich, the largest city in, and capital of, Bavaria, is a very interesting place to visit that is often overlooked by visitors to Germany. Not only does it have some very interesting attractions of its own, it is a good starting point for exploring the Bavarian Alps.

History

Bavaria was an independent state for centuries before it became part of the German Empire in 1871. Bavaria had been ruled for over 700 years by the Wittelsbach family, who had overseen the town plan of Munich and had many fine buildings erected. Even today, the people of this area think of themselves first as Bavarians, then as Germans.

Tourist Information

The Munich Tourist Office, 1 Sendlinger Strasse 1, 80331, Munich, ✆(089) 2333 0234, fax 2333 0337 (✉www.muenchen-tourist.de).

There is a tourist information office at the Railway Station, platform 2, that is ⊙open Mon-Sat 8am-8pm, Sun 10am-6pm; and another at the Town Hall in the Marienplatz.

Local Transport

Munich has an excellent public transport system that incorporates train, underground, trams and buses. It is best to enquire at one of the information offices about timetables and methods of buying tickets and passes. There are plenty of ticket machines available, but these can be difficult to use if you don't understand the instructions, so get that advice.

Accommodation

Prices given are for a double room per night with an ensuite, and are in the local currency. Major credit cards are accepted at these establishments. Rooms are airconditioned and central heating is the norm. Prices are higher during Oktoberfest and conventions in September. The area code for Munich is 089.

Hotel Europäischer Hof, Bayerstrasse 31, D-80335 München, ℂ89-55 1510, fax 89-55 15 1222, email ✎info@heh.de. 150 rooms, three tiers of accommodation. The hotel has a high quality collection of paintings, from Van Gogh and Picasso to Gaughin. There is a breakfast room and restaurant. It is modern, comfortable and located across the road from the Hauptbanhof (central railway) and airport shuttle - standard room ✪216-306DM.

Hotel Jedermann, Bayerstrasse 95, 80335 München, ℂ89-54 3240, fax 89-54 32 4111, ✪www.hotel-jedermann.de. 34 rooms, breakfast room, a smallish central hotel that is family owned and only a 5 minute walk from the Hauptbanhof - ✪130-240DM.

Arabella Sheraton Bogenhausen Hotel, Arabellastrasse 5, 81925 Bogenhausen, ℂ89-9 2320, fax 89-9232 4449. 644 rooms, shop, games room, nightclub, restaurants, lobby cafe and bar, fitness centre, swimming pool, parking, not located near the city, shuttle to the airport. Underground station is a 3 minute walk from the hotel then a 10 minute ride to the centre of the city. Near the new Munich

Exhibition Center. Parking available and taxi rank at the entrance - ✪280DM.

Hotel Splendid, Maximilianstrasse 54, 80538 München, ✆89-29 6606, fax 89-291 3176. 40 rooms. A small hotel that offers excellent service with very pleasant rooms. Great location near the Opera House with the underground station, Lehel, close by. There is a scenic terrace for drinks and breakfast - ✪182-322DM.

> ***Hotel Exquisit***
>
> Pettenkoferstrasse 3, 80336 München, ✆89- 55 1 9900, fax 89-55 19 9499, email ✉ info@hotel-exquisit.com. 50 rooms, garage, breakfast room, delightful inner courtyard, (though if you are renting a maisonette you may wish to have it on your own (✪340DM), which you may prefer over the impersonal atmosphere of a large international hotel). Located in a quiet side-street near Munich's centre. The Marienplatz, Stachus and Oktoberfest site can easily be reached on foot - ✪280-340DM.

Food and Drink

Bavarians eat a great deal of pork, so you won't see much in the way of beef or lamb dishes on the menu, but liberal use of the word 'schweine'. Also there will be more dumplings (which are rather delicious, although fattening) than potatoes. Sausages are a German favourite and the one associated with Munich is the Weisswurst, literally white sausage. It is made from a mixture of bacon and veal, parsley and pepper, and should be eaten with a sweet mustard.

The traditional Bavarian drink is beer, which comes in helles (light) or dunkels (dark). Special, stronger brews are made for important occasions, for example the Oktoberfest. If you can't stand the strong stuff, the word for 'shandy' is 'Radler'.

Sightseeing

A walking tour can start from the railway station.

Go along the extension of the platforms to the pedestrian zone, Schutzenstrasse, then Neuhauser Strasse and **St Michael's Church** (Michaelskirche). It is built in the Renaissance style, and is the crypt of the Wittelsbach family. The crypt is ⊙open Mon-Fri 10am-1pm, 2-4pm, Sat 10am-3pm.

Next stop is the **Frauenkirche**, the cathedral, which dates from the 15th century. It has twin towers capped with copper domes that are a city landmark, and the southern one has an elevator which only operates from ⊙April to October, Mon-Sat 10am-5pm, adults ✪4DM, children 2DM.

Nearby is **Marienplatz**, the centre of the city since its foundation in 1158. Here is the 15th century **Old Town Hall** (Rathaus) and the beautiful, Gothic-revival, 19th century **New Town Hall**, which has a mechanical show (automata) in the clock tower at ⊙11am each day, and from May to October also at noon, 5pm and 9pm. The tower of the new town hall is ☉open Mon-Fri 9am-7pm, Sat-Sun 10am-7pm, and the elevator ride is adult ✪3DM, child 1.50DM.

On the right, in Rindermarkt, is the **Peterskirche** (St Peter's), the oldest and most loved church in Munich. The tower called Alter Peter can be climbed and is ☉open Mon-Sat 9am-6pm, Sun 10am-6pm, adults ✪2.50DM, child 0.50DM.

Keep left from here and you will come to the **Victualienmarkt**, a large food and vegetable market. From here you can go two ways. Either keep going along Rosen Tal Strasse to the **Stadt Museum** on St Jakobs Plats (☉open Tues-Sun 10am-6pm), and then visit the **Asamkirche** in Sendinger Strasse, with its Bavarian Rococo creations, then along the Ring to Sendingertor Platz.

OR, go in the opposite direction along Sparkassen Strasse and on the right is the square with the famous **Hofbrauhaus**.

On the left is the **Alter Hof**, the first residence of the Wittelsbach rulers. Further along is Max Joseph Platz, with the **Nationaltheatre** (Opera House) and the **Residenz**, a complex of buildings that has grown over the centuries. Courtyards link the various buildings which include the **Residenzmuseum** with its fine art collection. It is ☉open Tues-Sun 10am-4.30pm. On the left is the **Feldherrnhalle**, built by Ludwig I in 1844 and copied from the Loggia dei Lanzi in Florence. And behind here on Odeons Platz is the **Theatinerkirche**, with its impressive dome and towers.

Once again there are choices to be made.

You can turn left into Brienner Strasse and go along to the **Platz der Opfer des Nationalsozialismus** (Square of the Victims of National Socialism), the area of the former Fuhrer and the Nazi party buildings. Then go past the obelisk covered in granite tiles to the Konigsplatz, which became the National Socialist Party's Square. On the northern side is the old **Glyptotek** (Greek and Roman sculptures, ☉open Tues,

Wed and Fri-Sun 10am-5pm, Thurs 10am-8pm), on the western side is a reproduction of the **Propylaon** on the Acropolis in Athens, and on the right hand side is **Lenbach House**. Once the home of the 19th century portrait artist, Franz von Lenbach, the house is now a gallery exhibiting a selection of his paintings as well as a fine collection of 19th century Munich landscape painters. It also has a good cafe and restaurant, and is ☉open Tues-Sun 10am-6pm. At the end of Brienner Strasse is Stiglmaier Platz with the Lowenbrau Keller and beer garden.

OR, you can go straight ahead along Ludwigsstrasse, which has the national library and St Ludwig's church on the right and the university on the left.

At Geschwister Scholl Platz, turn into Leopold Strasse and continue on to the Siegestor (victory arch), where the residential area of Schwabing begins. Near here is the **Cafe Stephanie** where great names of literature, such as Thomas Mann and Erich Muhsam, met for a bite, and where the postcard painter, Adolf Hitler began his career.

OR, if you turn right at Odeonsplatz and go across the **Hofgarten**, you will pass the art gallery that was built during the Third Reich and is an example of the architecture of that era. Continue past there and you will come to the very long and narrow **Englischer Garten**, which has a lake, a Greek temple, a Chinese pagoda, restaurants and cafes, and lots and lots of grass. To the left is **Schwabing**, the traditional students' quarter, but things are becoming a bit expensive there for them.

There are plenty of other interesting sights, but one that stands out is to the west of the city and that is **Schloss Nymphenburg**, the Baroque summer palace of the Bavarian royal family. It can be reached by U-Bahn to Rotkreuzplatz and then tram 12, and it is ☉open Tues-Sun 9am-12.30pm, 1.30-5pm April-Sept, 10am-12.30pm, 1.30-4pm Oct-March. There are guided tours, especially to Ludwig I's Gallery of Beautiful Women, and beautiful pavilions in the grounds.

Another place that may be of interest to some is **Dachau**. It can be reached by train, and has been preserved in memory of those people who were treated so inhumanely and who died there.

The Best of Munich in Brief

Old Town (Altstadt). The place for cafe's, churches, shopping and street entertainment of all kinds. Stroll through Mary's Square (Marienplatz) and take in the Gothic architecture and the Glockenspiel.

Alte Pinakothek. This is a huge museum with many important works. Over 900 paintings are on display spanning six centuries of the craft. *Barer Strasse 27.*

Neue Pinakothek. Located on the other side of the Square from the Alte Pinakothek, this museum pick up roughly where the other leaves off, in chronological terms. *Barer Strasse 29.*

Bavarian National Museum (Bayerisches Nationalmuseum). A great museum featuring much more than paintings. Many eras are covered in its three exhibition floors. *Prinzregentenstrasse 3.*

German Museum of Masterpieces of Science and Technology (Deutsches Museum). Dedicated to the history of technology with working displays and interactive exhibits. *Museumsinsel 1.*

Residenz. This is where Bavaria's rulers resided, collecting art and making architectural additions to their palace over the centuries, which accounts for the distinct variety of styles. Highlights of the complex are the Treasure House (Schatzkammer), Residenz Museum and Cuvillies Theatre, but the palace itself is generally considered poor by Europe's standards. *Max-Joseph-Platz 3.*

Nymphenburg Palace (Schloss Nymphenburg). Only slightly more interesting than the Residenz, Nymphenburg is where the Bavarian royalty, the Wittelsbach family, resided during the summer. The palace architecture is of the baroque style. *Schloss Nymphenburg 1.*

Cathedral of Our Lady (Frauenkirche). This gothic cathedral was built in the fifteenth century and destroyed during WWII bombings. After the war, the city's largest church was restored with impressive results to become Munich's most famous landmark.

St Michael's Church. A rare Renaissance church. *Neuhauser Strasse 52.*

St Peter's Church. Built in the twelfth century, this is the oldest church in Munich, with good views from its steeple. *Rindermarkt 1.*

Munich City Museum (Munchner Stadtmuseum). Four floors of very different collections. *St Jakob's Platz 1.*

Haus der Kunst. An interesting offering of modern twentieth century art. *Prinzregentenstrasse 1.*

English Garden (Englischer Garden). 3.7 square kilometres of landscaped gardens make this the biggest of its kind in Europe.

BMW Museum. Headquarters of the famous automobile manufacturer, with displays and tours. *Olympia-zentrum.*

Hofbrauhaus. Munich's largest beer hall, and indeed the world's best known, is open long hours every day and is very popular with tourists and locals alike. It has an astonishing capacity of 4,500 people.

Olympic Park and Stadium. The Olympic Games were held in these impressive grounds back in 1972. Apart from the stadium and swimming pool, there is a sports theme park worth visiting for its 40 interactive attractions.

Black Forest

Named for its gloomy interior, it is not difficult to imagine the Black Forest hiding the stuff of children's tales in its shadowy midst. Witch houses and dragon lairs would fit perfectly with this mythical landscape. At least, the Brothers Grimm thought so.

The *Schwarzwald*, occupying Germany's south west nook near the French border, is a beautiful region of lakes, waterfalls, mountains, charming folk, old world simplicity and, of course, dark forests. People come here mainly to hike and unwind.

Tourist Information

The main tourist offices for the area are in: Frieburg (Rotteckring 14, ✆0761 368 9090, 388 1882); Titisee (Strandbadstrasse 4, ✆980 40); St Margen (Town Hall, 91 1817); and Triberg (Kurhaus, ✆95 3230).

Best of The Black Forest In Brief

Baden-Baden. This town is on the northern outskirts of the Black Forest, and should be visited for its exquisite baths: a complex where you can enjoy pure pampering and personal luxury.

Titisee. This is a tourist magnet, attractive in its own right, but visitors should not make a stop here the highlight of their trip.

Schluchsee. Good hiking opportunities are available around the lake on which this town sits.

St. Margen. A pretty town with a photogenic waterfall and excellent hiking opportunities in its surrounds. Strap on your sturdy boots and get some healthy exercise in this picturesque environment.

St. Peter. This town is better noted for the enjoyable 7km trip to or from nearby St Margen, rather than for the destination itself.

Triberg. Visitors come here to see the spectacular waterfall, the highest in Germany.

Driving. The easiest way to explore the Black Forest is by hiring a car and taking a scenic drive between its towns.

Driving Through Germany

It is only possible to describe a few tours around Germany, as there are so many places to see.

The Rhine and Moselle Valleys
Itinerary - 5 Days - Distance 660kms

From Frankfurt, drive south to **Darmstadt**. This town is a cultural and art centre. There are many interesting museums, and a pretty artist's quarter. Further south, drive through **Heppenheim** with its 11th century observatory ruins, to **Heidelberg**, a university town in the Neckar Valley. In the ruins of the castle dating from the 14th century, concerts are held during the summer. Heading west from Heidelberg you reach **Bad Durkheim**, noted for its spa, and centre of the largest wine growing region in Germany. The biggest wine festival in Germany is here every September. North west of Bad Durkheim is **Idar Oberstein**, a town in a narrow valley. This town is well known for its jewellery trade.

Bernkastel-Kues, **Traben-Trarbachr** and **Zell** are important wine growing centres on the Moselle river. North through the Moselle

Old Roman Fort, near Frankfurt

Valley you come to **Bonn**, a major city. Bonn was the capital of the Federal Republic, and has many historic buildings. Beethoven was born here, and his house is open to the public. From Bonn, head south east to **Neuwied**, a town founded by religious refugees, and now known for its pumice industry. **Koblenz** nearby, is at the junction of the Rhine and Moselle rivers. This town is the commercial heart of the wine industry. Koblenz also has a famous wine festival in August. Along the Rhine, **Lahnstein** and **Braubach** are old towns with historic buildings. **St Goar** and **St Goarshausen** stand on opposite banks of the Rhine, and are linked by ferry. Castles overlook these towns. **Kaub** also has historic castles nearby, with the Pflaz Fortress on an island in the middle of the river. **Rudesheim** is a popular tourist destination, set near the Rheingau vineyards and the Rhine Gorge. There is a wine making museum in the castle.

Heading back towards Frankfurt, you pass through **Weisbaden** and **Mainz**. Weisbaden is noted for its spas, cultural facilities, parks and gardens. Mainz is an old industrial and university city with historic buildings and a printing museum. The tour finishes in **Frankfurt**, which is one of Germany's most important cities. It is situated on the river Main, and is known for its Motor Show and other trade fairs.

The Black Forest

Itinerary - 6 Days - Distance 682kms

From Stuttgart, head south to **Tubingen**, an old university town, situated on the Neckar river. **Hechingen** and **Sigmaringen** are pretty towns with ancient castles. Further south, you reach **Lindau** which is built out into Lake Constance (the **Bodensee**). It is joined to the mainland by the Sea Brucke, and is a popular tourist destination. Driving along the northern shore of Lake Constance you pass through the holiday towns of **Friedrichs-Hafen** and **Meersburg**, which are very picturesque. At **Unter-Uhldingen** you can see reconstructions of Stone and Bronze Age buildings.

By making a short detour into Switzerland, you can see the spectacular waterfall (rheinfalls) at **Neuhausen**. The best place to see this sight is from the grounds of the Laufen Castle. Back into Germany, **Titisee** is a popular sporting town. It is near Mt Feldberg, the highest peak in the Black Forest.

Freiburg is the largest town in the Black Forest region, and is noted for its university and historic buildings. Driving north from Freiburg, you pass through the health spas of **Alpirsbach**, **Freudenstadt**, and the famous **Baden-Baden**. As well as the spas, there are many other things to see and do here, including visiting the Casino, the vineyards or taking a cable car up the nearby mountain. Heading back towards Stuttgart is **Pforzheim**, the gateway to the Black Forest, and well known for its jewellery and watch making industry. **Stuttgart** is the largest city in the south west of Germany, and as well as being a commercial centre is also very scenic.

Germany from West to East

Itinerary - 3 Days - Distance 240kms

From the Dutch border drive east. **Osnabruck** is notable for its cathedral, dating from medieval times. Further east you arrive at

Hannover, another old city. Hannover is an important art and cultural centre, with many galleries and museums. Of note is the Herrenhausen Palace, with its gardens. **Braunschweig**, and **Magdeburg** feature castles and cathedrals from the 12th and 13th century, as well as some examples of Roman architecture.

Driving towards Berlin, you pass through **Brandenburg**, which although is a modern city, has many ancient manuscripts held in the cathedral. **Potsdam** is a very scenic city, with castles, parks and galleries well worth visiting. From Potsdam, you reach **Berlin**. There are many things to see and do in this city, now the capital of Germany. As well as the ruins of the Berlin Wall, there are many galleries, historic buildings and palaces to see.

South of Berlin, **Wittenberg** and **Dessau**, lies Worlitz Nature Park on Warlitz Lake. Dessau is the home of the Bauhaus movement, and has a museum dedicated to design. Many of the buildings have been restored. Heading south from Dessau you reach **Leipzig**, a famous university, publishing and cultural centre.There is much to see and do here. Through **Merseburg**, you reach **Halle**, Handel's birthplace, and you can visit the cathedral where he played. The tour finishes here, and you can either explore more of Germany or head into the Czech Republic.

Austria

LAND-LOCKED AUSTRIA is situated in Central Europe and has an area of 83,849 sq km. It is a democratic federal republic of nine provinces, with a total population of 8,000,000. The capital is Vienna, where approximately a fifth of the population live, and the language of the country is German.

Austria is very mountainous with peaks reaching up to 3800m. It is a popular skiing venue with snow from January to the end of April in some parts.

Climate

Austria has a moderate climate, temperatures varying according to altitude. Generally winter extends from December to March, and average temperatures are 24C in July and 1C in January.

Entry Regulations

Visitors must have a valid passport, but a visa is not required for visits of up to three months (six months for holders of European passports).

The duty free allowance for travellers over 17 years of age from non-European countries is 200 cigarettes or 50 cigars or 250 grams of tobacco, 2 litres of wine and 1 litre of spirits. The tobacco allowance for travellers from European countries is 400 cigarettes or 100 cigars or 500 grams of tobacco. Non-Europeans are entitled to these if they have *stayed* in Europe prior to travelling to Austria. Changing planes or spending time in a transit lounge does not count as a stay.

There is no restriction on the import or export of local or foreign currencies. No vaccinations are required for any international traveller.

Currency

The Euro will be introduced in January 2002. The previous currency of the land was the Austrian Schilling (AS), divided into 100 Groschen. Approximate exchange rates, which should be used as a guide only, are as follows.

1 Euro = 13.7603 Schillings
A$ = 7.86AS
Can$ = 9.70AS
NZ$ = 6.36AS
S$ = 8.31AS
UK£ = 22.20AS
US$ = 15.26AS

Notes are in denominations of 5000, 1000, 500, 100, 50 and 20 Schillings, and coins are 20, 10, 5 and 1 Schillings, and 50 and 10 Groschen.

Shopping

Banks are generally ⊕open 8am-12.30pm, 1.30-3pm Mon, Tues, Wed and Fri, 8am-12.30pm, 1.30-5.30pm Thurs. All banks are closed Sat and Sun. Exchange counters at airports and the main railway stations are usually ⊕open 8am-8pm (Vienna until 10pm) daily.

Shopping hours are ⊕Mon-Fri 8am-6pm, Sat 8am-1pm, although many stay open until 5pm. Many shops close for two hours in the middle of the day.

Credit cards are widely accepted in the major cities, but not in the smaller towns even at petrol stations.

Telephone

International direct dialling is available and the International code is 00, the country code 43. The area code for Vienna is 01 or 09, that for Salzburg is 0662. Payphones have slots that take 1, 5, 10 and 20 schilling coins, and an audible tone warns that time is running out.

It is expensive to make international calls from hotels, particularly in Vienna where there is often a surcharge of 200% of the cost of the call.

Driving

An International Driving Licence is necessary to hire a car, and third party insurance is obligatory. It is compulsory to wear a seat-belt, and children under 12 years of age are not permitted in front seats.

Speed limits are:

Cars

built-up areas	-	50kph
open roads	-	100kph
motorways	-	130kph

Cars with Trailer over 750kg

open roads	-	60kph
motorways	-	70kph

You should expect to pay tolls on expressways, multi-lane highways and city highways.

Miscellaneous

Local time is GMT + 1 (Central European Time) with daylight saving in force from late March to late September.

Electricity - 220v AC, with round, two-pin plugs.

Health - Austria has good health services but they are very expensive. It is recommended that visitors have adequate medical insurance.

Sales Tax (VAT) - Citizens of non-European countries who purchase goods in excess of AS1000 in one store at one time can apply for a refund of the VAT they paid. Ask the shopkeeper to complete the tax-free cheque form, and present it, along with the merchandise, to customs officials upon leaving the country by air or by car and travelling into a country that is not part of the European Union. People travelling by train should send their purchases as registered luggage, then the customs clerk at the railway station at point of departure will validate the tax-free cheque. More information can be obtained at any Tourist Information Office.

Vienna

Gateway to eastern Europe and capital of Austria, Vienna (Wien) lies on the banks of the Danube, near the borders of Hungary, Slovakia and Czechia.

It is very much a city of music, having been home to such composers as Mozart, Bruckner, Beethoven, Schubert, Brahms, Haydn and Johann Strauss.

History

The site of Vienna was occupied by the Celts long before the birth of Christ, and it was known to have been a Roman military camp called Vindobona in the year 1AD.

In 1155, the Babenbergs, the first dynasty to reign over Austria, chose Vienna as their residence. During the reigns of Leopold V and Leopold VI, the city underwent considerable expansion, financed in part by the ransom the English were forced to pay the Babenbergs for the return of their captured King Richard the Lionheart.

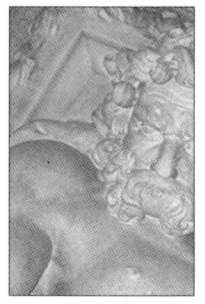

Rudolf I of Habsburg took control of Austria after victory in the Battle of Durnkrut in 1278, but the people were not too thrilled about him and subsequently rebelled. However, it is the Habsburgs that Vienna has to thank for her reputation as one of the great cities of the world - particularly Charles VI and Maria Theresia in the 18th century and Francis Joseph in the 19th.

Tourist Information

Tourist information offices are located at 38 Karntner Strasse (Opera House), and 40 Obere Augarten Strasse, ✆(01) 211 14-222, fax (01) 216 84 92 (www.info.wien.at).

Local Transport

Vienna has an excellent public transport system. The U-Bahn (underground railway) has three lines, and there are bus, trolley and rail services to all parts of the city.

For an interesting way to visit the old parts of the city, hire a *fiaker* and listen to the driver's tales of Viennese life in olden days. Allow plenty of time.

Worth looking into is **The Vienna Card (Die Wien Karte)** which costs ✪AS210 and offers 72 hours travel on the underground, buses or trams, reduced entry fees to several attractions, and discounts on guided tours, shopping, and meals in certain cafes, taverns and restaurants. The Card is available at most hotels, Transport and Information Offices, or outside Vienna with credit card by phone ✆43-1-798 44 00-28.

Accommodation

Following is a small selection of hotels in Vienna, with prices for a double room per night, which should be used as a guide only. The telephone area code is 01.

City, Bauernmarkt 10, 1010 Wien, ✆01/533 9521, fax 01/535 5216. A pension on the third floor of the building which offers 19 plainly

Vienna

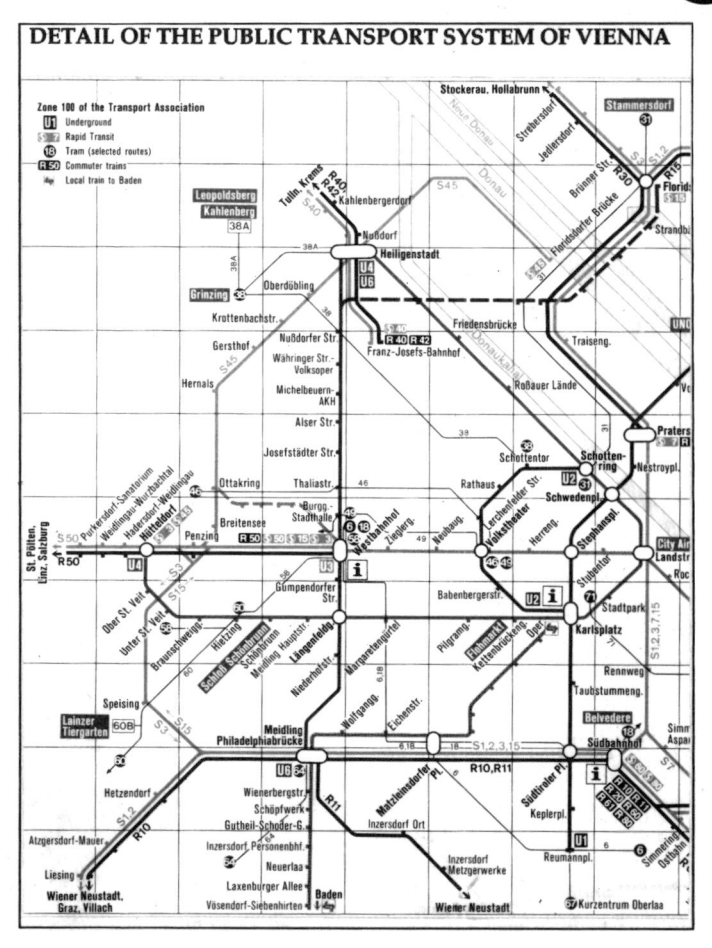

DETAIL OF THE PUBLIC TRANSPORT SYSTEM OF VIENNA

furnished rooms well located in the old part of the city. All you can eat breakfast included in the price of the room. Cheaper in winter - ✪from 990S.

Kugel, Siebensterngasse 43/Neubaugasse 46, 1070 Wien, ✆01/523 3355, fax 01/523 3355. A run down family owned hotel of 38 rooms located just to the west of the ring (old city). Continental breakfast included in the price of the room, but no credit cards are accepted - ✪780S.

Hotel Karntnerhof, Grashofgasse 4, A-1010 Vienna, ✆01/512 1923, fax 01/513 22 28 33. A comfortable small hotel advertising itself as family friendly and located a few minutes walk from the cathedral. 44 rooms, some available without private bathroom for a substantial saving (double without bathroom ✪860S). Breakfast is included - ✪1,720S.

Hotel Cryston, Gaudenzdorfer Gürtel 65, (✉cryston@hotels.or.at). 3-star hotel with individually furnished rooms. Centrally located, close to public transport and a short trip to the Ring and the Old Town - ✪990AS (73E).

Hotel Royal, Singerstrasse 3, A-1010 Vienna, ✆01/51 568, fax 01/513 9698. A pleasant hotel furnished with reproduction antiques, good-sized rooms and all the comforts of a decent, though not expensive hotel. St Stephens Cathedral is nearby and some rooms have views overlooking it - ✪from 1,600S.

Hotel Schneider, Getreidemarkt 5, A-1060 Vienna, ✆01/588 380, fax 01/588 38 212. A good choice for families as suites contain kitchenettes. The hotel is well appointed, tastefully decorated and centrally located. A buffet breakfast is included - ✪from 1,750S.

Hilton Vienna, Am Stadtpark, ✆717 00-0, fax 713 06 91 (✉rm_vienna@hilton.com). A deluxe hotel in the downtown area. Facilities include restaurants, bars, coffee shop, health club and shops - ✪3100-3700AS (225-268E).

Holiday Inn Crowne Plaza Vienna, Handelskai 269, ✆727 77, fax 727 77-199 (✉crowneplaza@aon.at). A superior first class hotel. Facilities include restaurants, bars, coffee shop, health club, sauna and shops - ✪1970-2550AS (144-185E).

Parkhotel Schoenbrunn, Hietzinger Hauptstrasse 10-20, ✆878 04, fax 878 04-3220 (✎parkhotel.schoenbrunn@austria-trend.at). A first class hotel in the midtown area. Facilities include restaurants, bars, coffee shop, health club, swimming pool, shops and a beauty salon - ✪1700-2950AS (124-215E).

> *Hof Hotel Wien*
>
> Kulmgasse 22, 1-488-05, (fax) 1-488-05-8 (✎hof@hotels.or.at). This modern 4-star hotel is located between the Schonbrunn Palace and Grinzing - ✪1590 (116E).

For those on a budget there are the following **Youth Hostels**:
Jugendgasterhaus Wien Brigittenau, Friedrich Engelsplatz 24, ✆(1) 330 0598, fax (1) 330 8379.
Jugendherberge Wien, Myrthengasse 7, Neustiftgasse 85, ✆(1) 523 63160, fax (1) 523 5849.
Hostel Ruthensteiner, Robert Hameringgasse 24, ✆(1) 893 4202, fax (1) 893 2796 (✎hostel.ruthensteiner@telecom.at).

Food and Drink

The most famous dish from this city is Wiener Schnitzel, but there are many more national dishes to tempt the taste buds, including various types of sausage.

Any stay in Vienna should include a visit to a Coffee House, and one of the best known is **Sacher**, Philharmonikerstrasse 4, ✆51 456-0 (✎hotel@sacher.com), home of the Sachertorte that has found its way onto menus all over the world. The Sacher is hopen daily 5pm-midnight.

Your hotel, or the Tourist Information Office, can provide you with a booklet listing over 100 coffee houses in the city, and you are sure to find something that appeals.

In the suburbs of Grinzing, Sioevering, Heiligenstadt and Nussdorf, a cluster of fir twigs hanging above the door of an inn means that the year's wine is ready to be enjoyed. These are known as Heurigen localities, and the wine can only be from the innkeeper's own vineyards. There is also Heurigen music to accompany the wine and food, and it usually consists of a quartet of two violins, an accordion and a guitar, who play traditional Schrammel tunes. It is great fun, and very popular with the locals.

Sightseeing

The Ring is an avenue that was created after the city wall was removed in 1857. It has several names as it circles the old city - Schotten Ring, Dr Karl Lueger Ring, Dr Karl Renner Ring, and so on.

The **Stock Exchange** is on Schotten Ring, and to the south are the main buildings of the **University**, the new Gothic **Rathaus** (Town Hall - guided tours available), and opposite is the famous **Burg Theatre** (Palace Theatre - guided tours available).

To the south is the much-loved **Volksgarten** (people's gardens) with the **Theseus Temple**. On the other side of the Ring is **Parliament House**, which is built like a Greek temple. In front of the building is a monumental fountain topped by a 14m statue of Pallas Athene, and the poles on each side of the fountain fly flags when parliament is sitting. When there are no flags guided tours are available. It is a very photogenic building. Next are the **Alte Hofburg** and the **Neue Hofburg** (Old and New Imperial Palaces) on Helden Platz, the seat of the Habsburg family and centre of a world empire. Nowadays they are open to the public and contain the **National Library** and the **Ethnological Museum**.

In Michaeler Platz, in the direction of the city, is the **Looshaus** and unsurpassed views of the sprawling Old Hofburg. Also in the Hofburg is the world famous **Spanish Riding School** whose Lipizzaner horses have morning work-outs ☉late Feb-June, Sept-Dec (10am), and tickets are available at the entrance. At the end of the Hofburg is the **Albertina** which houses the world's largest collection of graphic arts. Near here in Philharmoniker Strasse is the famous **Hotel Sacher** which sells the original Sacher's Torte.

Turn left and walk along Neuer Markt to the **Kapuziner Church** and the **Habsburg Crypt**, which contains the sarcophagi of 147 members of the royal family, including twelve emperors and sixteen empresses. The tomb of the beloved Maria Theresia is considered by some to be one of the most beautiful examples of rococo art.

Go through the **Burgtor** (gate) and cross the Ring to the **Natural History Museum** and **Museum of Fine Arts**, both of which started off with the emperors' collections. In the middle of the park between the two buildings is the **Maria Theresia** memorial. Along the Opern Ring behind the New Hofburg are the Hofburg Gardens which have many memorials: Emperor Franz Joseph, Mozart, Goethe and others.

From here it is just a short walk to the **Opera House** the first of the monumental buildings erected on the Ring. Although it is very much the centre of cultural life in Vienna, it was not well received either during its construction or upon its completion. Built in the French Renaissance style, people likened it to a railway station and made other derogatory statements to the point where one of the architects committed suicide. The opera house opened on May 25, 1869, with a presentation of Mozart's *Don Giovanni*. Guided tours are available.

Following Karntner Strasse from the Opera House towards St Stephen's Cathedral, the main shopping area is on the left, and it stretches past Neuer Markt to Kohl-markt. The streets here are pedestrian malls, and contain a wide variety of shops from up-market boutiques to souvenir stalls. There are also many coffee shops and restaurants.

St Stephen's Cathedral was originally consecrated in 1147, and was a Romanesque structure. The Gothic reconstruction commenced in 1304, and was consecrated 36 years later. At the end of the 16th century a Renaissance-style octagonal capped roof and a belfry were added. It is one of the great churches of Europe and well worth a visit.

Sights Further Afield

The **Belvedere Palace** is situated on a rise south of the city centre. It was built for Prince Eugene of Savoy at the beginning of the 18th century, and is a masterpiece of sophisticated Baroque architecture. Prince Eugene played a major part in Vienna's liberation from the Turks, and consequently became very popular with the Emperor and the local people. The Emperor had the Belvedere built in gratitude, and the local people made sure the Prince kept control of the army when he was threatened with dismissal.

The State Treaty that released Austria from its 10 years of occupation by the four Allied powers was signed in the Belvedere Palace on May 15, 1955. The upper belvedere can be reached from Prinz Eugen Strasse and the Gurtel, and it has a gallery of 19th and 20th century paintings, including works by Gustav Klimt and Egon Schiele. (☉Open Tues-Sun 10am-5pm, ✆795 57-134). The lower belvedere is off the Rennweg. There you will find a museum of medieval and baroque art.

The **Schonbrunn Palace** is on the west side of the city, and is one of Vienna's most famous sights. The name means 'beautiful fountains' after those that were built over the natural springs in the 17th century, when the Emperor Matthias had his hunting lodge on the site. The lodge was burnt down by the Turks in 1863, and Leopold I decided to build a new summer residence for his family. The Gloriette (triumphal arches) was completed in 1775, and was used in those days for innumerable social events.

The palace was the favourite residence of Maria Theresia, whose daughter Marie Antoinette, of French Revolution fame, spent her childhood here. Mozart performed here for the Empress at the age of six. Napoleon had his headquarters here in the early 1800s, and his son, whose mother was Archduchess Marie-Louise, was raised here by his grandfather Emperor Franz. Emperor Franz Josef was born here and died here, after 68 years on the throne, and it was at Schonbrunn that Emperor Karl I abdicated, bringing an end to 636 years of Habsburg rule.

Today 40 rooms of the palace are open to the public and are not to be missed. Allow plenty of time for a visit as there is so much to take in, and time is needed to wander through the gardens, and visit the Gloriette for a magnificent view of the city.

The Best of Vienna in Brief

Hofburg Palace. The winter home of the Habsburgs has 2,600 rooms and an amazing history of survival since its construction in 1279. Within the complex is the famous Spanish Riding School and its Lippizaner stallions.

Museum of Fine Arts (Kunsthistorisches Museum). Displays the stunning art collection amassed by the Habsburg family along with additional ancient and classical pieces. *Maria-Theresien-Platz, Burgring 5*.

Augustinian Church (Augustinerkirche). Built in the 14th century, this church was the venue for imperial weddings. Its architecture underwent a reverse transformation from baroque back to its original gothic style. *Augustinerstrasse 3*.

Lipizzaner Museum. The Spanish Riding School in Vienna attracts hundreds of thousands of visitors each year who marvel at the classic equestrian skills (dating back four hundred years) of the riders and their steeds. Visit the Lipizzaner Museum in the Renaissance building to see its collection of uniforms and paintings which trace the history of the horses. Then move on to the stables themselves. *Reitschulgasse 2*.

Kaisergruft. This crypt contains 147 bodies from the Habsburg family, with details of the family tree and tombs with intruiging artwork. *Neuer Markt*.

Vienna Boys' Choir. Performances during the Sunday morning mass at the Palace Chapel (Die Burgkapelle) in Hofburg.

Opera (Staatsoper). An inherent part of Vienna's history and culture. Each year there are over 300 performances here, offering plenty of opportunties for you to immerse yourself in the atmosphere. *Opernring 2*.

St. Stephan's Cathedral (Dompfarre St. Stephan). A magnificent restored gothic building with a 450-foot-high steeple. A visit is essential. *Stephansplatz 1*.

Carinthia Street (Karntnerstrasse). This pedestrian street is known for its shopping and sidewalk entertainment.

The Danube. Seeing the river on a cruise or while cycling leisurely along its shores are two relaxing delights.

Academy of Fine Arts (Gemaldegalerie Akademie der Bildenden Kunste). Houses Bosch's *Last Judgement* and works by Botticelli and Rembrandt. *Schillerplatz 3*.

Wine Tasting. Vienna Woods is the place to sample the freshly-produced wines from the *heurigen* (wine taverns) dotted across the vineyards overlooking the Danube Valley.

Schonbrunn Palace. Summer residence of the Habsburgs whose stunning architecture and interior decoration rivals but does not quite surpass Versailles. *Schonbrunner Schlosstrasse*.

Salzburg

The beautiful city of Salzburg is the capital of the province of the same name, and has a population of 145,000. The picturesque Salzach River flows through the centre of the city, which is famous as the birthplace of the composer Wolfgang Amadeus Mozart. It also was the location for the movie classic *The Sound of Music*, as the Trapp family were residents of Salzburg.

The old town is on the left side of the Salzach, dominated by the Fortress Hohensalzburg; the new town on the right of the river nestles beneath the Kapuzinerberg (the Capuchin monastery/fortress).

History

Historians agree that parts of Salzburg were inhabited as far back as 3000 BC. At various times during its history the town was home to Illyrians, Celts, and then Romans, who called it Juvavum. The town became an important trade centre, and was raised by the Romans to the status of a municipium, but during the migration of Germanic tribes, the settlement was destroyed.

It was the 7th century that saw the beginnings of today's city, when Bishop Rupertus founded the Benedictine monastery of St Peter,

View of the Alstadt (Old Town)

which became the seat of the bishops, later archbishops, for many centuries. The first cathedral was erected by Bishop Virgil in the 8th century, and work on the present cathedral began in 1614 under Archbishop Markus Sitticus.

This religious importance has resulted in a wealth of ecclesiastic architecture, as well as palaces, museums and many interesting period houses.

Tourist Information

The information office is in Mozartplatz, and has all the information, maps, brochures, etc, that are available, ✆(662) 889 87-330 (👁www.salzburginfo.or.at)

Local Transport

The city has a good public transport system, but for the visitor walking tours are the way to go. If you run out of energy in the old city, continue your tour in a fiaker (horse-drawn cab). Their starting point is in the Residenzplatz.

Accommodation

Following is a small selection of accommodation venues, with prices for a double room per night, which should be used as a guide only. Usually a continental breakfast is included in the room rates. The telephone area code is 662.

Kobenzi-Vitalhotel, Am Gaisberg 11, ©641 510, fax 642 238 (✏info@hotel-kobenzi.co.at). A superior first class hotel in the midtown area. Facilities include restaurant, bar, health club, swimming pool, shops and beauty salon - ✪2200-5900AS.

Stadtkrug, Linzer Gasse 20, ©873 545, fax 873 545-54 (✏lucian@ping.at). A first class hotel in the midtown area. Facilities include restaurant, bar and swimming pool - ✪1600-2450AS.

Markus Sittikus, Markus-Sittikus-Strasse 20, ©871 121-0, fax 871 121-58 (✏markus-sittikus@austria.at). A medium range hotel in the midtown area - ✪980-1400AS.

Lechner, Rainerstrasse 11, ©872 740, fax 879 380. A budget hotel, but close to most things - ✪880-990AUS.

There are several **Youth Hostels** in Salzburg:
Jugendgastehaus Salzburg, Josef-Preis Allee 18, ©842 6700, fax 841 101 (✏oejhv-sbg-jgh-nonntal@oejhv.or.at).
Eduard-Heinrich Haus, Eduard Heinrich Strasse 2, ©625 976, fax 627 980.
Haunspergstrasse, Haunspergstrasse 27, ©875 030, fax 883 477.

Food and Drink

Coffee houses and restaurants abound in Salzburg, especially along the banks of the Salzach. The city even has its own special dish - Salzburger Nockerin which translates roughly as 'souffle style of Salzburg'. It is lemon-flavoured and delicious.

Sightseeing

A walking tour of the old city begins at the information office in Mozartplatz.

The platz has a large statue of Mozart, but apparently it is not true to life because his sons were not too impressed with the likeness when it was unveiled in 1842. The tour then winds its way to the **Alter Markt** (old market), a photogenic square formed by old houses that is home to: **St Florian's Fountain**; the **Smallest House of Salzburg**, now owned by an optician; **Cafe Tomaselli** (1703) the oldest coffee house in the city; and possibly a few stalls reminiscent of the square's original function.

The tour then enters the pedestrian Getreidegasse and passes the **old town hall** (1407), a suitably chastened McDonald's sign, and **burghers' houses** from the 15th to 18th centuries. Many little lanes and alleys run of the street near this section, and they contain interesting shops and coffee houses. Also note in this street, and many others in the old city, the hanging shingles outside the buildings. These are mostly descriptive of the profession or trade of the owner, and were designed before most people could read and write. Some of them are quite amusing.

The most visited house on Getreidegasse is no. 9, **Mozart Geburtshaus**, where Mozart was born on January 27, 1756, and lived until 1763. The house now contains a museum of Mozart memorabilia, including his childhood violin, many other instruments that he played, letters, manuscripts and more - very interesting. Salzburg is very proud of

Mozart and has several yearly events that celebrate his music - Mozart Week in late January, festivals at Easter and through all of August, and the famous Salzburger Kulturtage in October.

Continuing to the right at the end of Getreidegasse brings you to **Anton-Neumayr Platz**, where there is a statue of the Virgin Mary dating from 1691. On the left is the **Monchsberg lift**, which ascends inside the rock to a terrace that offers a fantastic view over the city. It is also the entrance to the **Cafe Winkler** and its gambling casino.

Next on the tour is Museumplatz, where there are a couple of museums, then around the corner is **St Mark's church** (1699). Follow the map for a few twists and turns then stop at the traffic lights on Sigmundsplatz to admire the **Horse-Pond**. The paintings on the rear wall were restored in 1916, but the main attraction is the *Horse Tamer* which was sculpted by Michael Bernhard Mandl in 1695.

The walk then visits Universitatsplatz, where there is a food market every day except Sunday, and the **Church of the Immaculata** (1707), which has to be one of the most beautiful Baroque churches. Follow directions to the Hofstallgasse and there is the **Festspielhaus** (playhouse), which is actually two playhouses, the new containing a 2000+ auditorium, and the old seating 1300 people. Nearby is the open galleried theatre that was the venue for tournaments and animal baiting in the olden days. Continue on into Franciskanergasse to the **Franciscan Church**, consecrated in 1223, and well worth a look-see. Exit by the south door and walk under an arch into the courtyard of **St Peter's Abbey**, founded in 690 by St Rupert. Be prepared now to be overwhelmed and educated as you wander from church to tomb to chapel, to cemetery to mausoleum, ending at **St Margaret's Chapel** with its beautifully cared-for graves.

Next stop is the **Hohensalzburg fortress** (1077) which can be reached by taking the funicular from its lower station in Festungsgasse. There are great panoramic views of the city from the fortress, but there are also interesting guided tours available that include the state apartments, the cells and torture chamber, and the fortress and Rainer museums.

The **Cathedral** (Dom) is in Domplatz and can seat 10,000 people. There have been several cathedrals on this site, and the present church was consecrated in 1628. The dome was completely destroyed and the interior badly damaged during World War II, so it was restored and reconsecrated in 1959. Its bells are the largest in Europe. The cathedral has much for those interested in art and sculpture, and there is a museum that was inaugurated on the 1200th anniversary of the cathedral that has an unusual collection of religious memorabilia. Heading now towards the Residenzplatz, watch out for the **Excavations Museum** which has artifacts found on the cathedral site that range from early Roman times to the Middle Ages.

Residenzplatz is the largest of Salzburg's squares and it contains the largest baroque fountain in the world. It is also home to the **Residence**, completed in 1619 and the seat of the archbishops until 1803. Conducted tours are offered and it is the best way to view the place. The building contains some wonderful works of art.

On the other side of the square is the **New Residence**, erected in 1602. It has the **Glockenspiel Tower** which plays works by Mozart every day at ☉7am, 11am and 6pm.

The only place left on this walking tour is **St Michael's Church** on the north side of Residenzplatz. It dates from the year 800 and is the oldest parish church in the city.

It might be a good idea to take time out now to enjoy a stroll along the river before crossing one of the bridges over the Salzach to the new town.

First stop is the **Mirabell gardens**, which are very formally laid out and include a large fountain with sculptures that are supposed to represent the four elements. At one end of the gardens stands what's left of the **Schloss Mirabell**, which was mostly destroyed by fire in 1818.

In the Makartplatz is the **Landestheater**; next door is the **Salzburg Marionette Theatre**; adjacent is the **Mozarteum**, an international music academy; outshining them all is the **Church of the Holy Trinity**; and just off the square in Theatergasse is the **Cafe Bazar**, which is a popular artists' haunt. There are two more churches in this area - **St Sebastian's** in the Linzergasse, and the **Loreto Church** in Paris-Lodron Strasse.

Finally, there is the **Capuchin Monastery**, and a magnificent panoramic view is available from the bastion below the monastery.

The Best of Salzburg in Brief

Mozart's Birthplace (Mozart Gerburtshaus). Home of the Mozart family, containing valuable art and instruments used by the young musical genius. *Getreidegasse 9*.

Mozart Residence (Mozart Wohnhaus). The original house was destroyed during WWII and this replica was built and opened as a musem in 1996. It is the place to go for a complete record of Mozart's life and work. *Makartplatz 8*.

Salzburg Cathedral. One of Salzburg's gems, this 17th century marvel presents an unmatched testament to Renaissance architecture, with a baroque interior that takes in the best of this style. The cathedral's organ has no fewer than four thousand pipes. *Residenzplatz, south*.

Stiftskirche St. Peter. Another church crafted in the baroque style, this former Romanesque basilica contains a wealth of art. *St-Peter-Bezirk*.

Glockenspiel. Head into Mozartplatz to hear the 35 bells of this carillon ring out their tunes three times daily. *Mozartplatz 1*.

Mirabell Gardens. A combination of natural features and man-made figures carefully arranged by Fischer von Erlach spread across this public park. *Off Markatplatz*.

Part of the Mirabell Gardens

Mirabell Palace (Shloss Mirabell). After all the architectual changes that have been made in rebuilding the palace, not much of the original is left to appreciate. *Mirabell Square*.

Getreidegasse. This is the expensive but visually-attractive shopping district of Salzburg.

Residenz. Apart from its rich and fabulous State rooms, this old palace of the Archbishops is also famous for its large and lavish baroque fountain and for the fact that Mozart often entertained guests here with his music. *Residenzplatz 1*.

Museum Carolino Augusteum. An interesting collection of various pieces spanning archaeological rarities to Romantic-period paintings. *Museumplatz 1.*

Sound of Music Tour. Filmed on location, this classic film brought some of Austria's best scenery to the silver screen. Popular tours take you to all the sites - from the mansion to the gazebo - which have been burnt into your memory by endless re-runs.

Monchsberg. Good views back over Salzburg can be enjoyed from this natural ridge bearing old defence fortifications.

Hohensalzburg Fortress. Complete construction of this impregnable stronghold took a staggering 604 years. The castle is still preserved in its entirety. Highlights include the medieval art, the torture chamber, the residential quarters of the Archbishops, and the best views over Salzburg, which on a clear day stretch all the way to the Alps. *Monchsberg 34.*

Innsbruck

Ringed by snow-capped peaks and filled with gothic architecture, the beautiful town of Innsbruck in western Austria welcomes the marvelling traveller. About 5 million visitors tread the cobblestone streets every year, breathing the crisp alpine air and making preparations for a rewarding hike or a ski trip to the powdery Tyrolean slopes nearby. Innsbruck is one of the top attractions in Austria.

Tourist Information

The tourist office, at Burggraben 3, ✆0512-59850, is ⏰open 8am-6pm on weekdays and in the morning on Sundays. Enquire about accommodation, hiking tours and skiing packages.

Accommodation

Innsbruck has plenty of accommodation options, from five star opulence to budget hostels. Below are details of two hotels in the middle range, with prices for a double room per night.

Hotel Neue Post, Maximilianstrasse15, ✆59 4 76, fax 58 18 18, ✎email: innsbruck@hotel-neue-post.at. Over a century old, this family-owned four star hotel is housed in a classic European building with a central location. There are 60 rooms, some recently renovated, which are comfortable and quite spacious - ✪1700ATS including breakfast.

Goldener Adler, Herzog-Friedrichstrasse 6, ✆571 1110, fax 584 409, ✎email office@goldeneradler.com. This historic inn has 33 rooms with modern, elegant furnishings and all the modern conveniences. Pay a little extra for a view of the Alstadt. The restaurant serves traditional Tyrolean cuisine. Located in the centre of the Old Town, the Goldener is perfect for sightseeing - ✪880ATS.

Best of Innsbruck In Brief

Old Town (Altstadt). The quaint medieval part of town in the centre of Innsbruck, most famous for its Golden Roof: a balcony covered in gold tiles that was once the 'ringside seat' occupied by Maximilian I whenever something took place in the

Altstadt, Innsbruck

square below that deserved his royal attention. Take your time strolling through this charming quarter.

Folk Museum. Delve into the lives and culture of the Tyrol people over the centuries. *Universitatstrasse 2*.

Maria-Theresa-Strasse. The highlights of this main street are St Anna's Column (Annasaule), the Triumphal Arch (Triumphforte) and the Town Hall (Rathaus). *City centre*.

Hofburg. Maximilian used this palace as his residence in the fifteenth century. Paintings of the Habsburg family can be viewed inside on a guided tour. *Rennweg 1*.

Hofkirche. Contains an extravagent monument to Maxilimilian I and 28 bronze statues. *Universitatstrasse 2*.

Lookouts. Take one of the many mountain lifts for unbeatable alpine views overlooking Innsbruck and the greater Tyrol region. It is not difficult to see why Innsbruck continues to draw visitors in their millions every year.

Driving Through Austria

A Scenic Tour of Austria by Road

Itinerary - 7 Days - Distance 760kms

Enter from Switzerland at **Feldkirch**, with its medieval market square. From the west to get to the rest of the country, travel through the **Alberg**. You can take the toll tunnel or drive over the pass to **St Anton**. In winter this is one of the world's top ski areas, in summer a delightful holiday centre. Travelling further east towards **Ehrwald** is an area known as **Ausserfern**. This is ideal for hiking and cycling. Driving towards **Innsbruck** you pass through **Seefeld**, a resort area. The Brenner pass and the Achen pass provide entry into Austria from the north. The Achen pass leads down to **Jenbach**, where a steam cogwheel train runs in summer.

Through the Brixen valley, you reach **Kitzbuhel**, another famous resort, then drive down to **Zell Am See**, a historic mountain town by the lake. The Salzach river takes you towards **Salzburg**, through the Gastein valley and the ski/spa resorts of **Bad Hogastein** and **Badgastein**. **Eisriesenwelt** has the largest ice cave system in the world while **Hallein** has a working salt mine where visitors can tour the mine.

From Salzburg, head towards **Gmunden**, passing through **St Wolfgang** and **Bad Ischl**. At Gmunden you can take the expressway towards Vienna, detouring at **Melk**. This part of Austria is known as the Wachau, an extremely scenic and historic section of the country. The **Danube** between **Melk** and **Krems** is picturesque. From here, you can head towards **Vienna** through **Stockerau**.

Switzerland

LAND-LOCKED SWITZERLAND has an area of 41,288 sq km and a population of around 6,675,000 people, whose language depends on which part of the country they inhabit. Around 70% speak a dialect of German, but those who live between the French border and the Matterhorn speak French, and account for another 20%. The remaining 10% is divided between the southern-most Canton of Ticino where Italian is spoken, and the Engadine and Upper Rhine Valley where people speak Romansch, an ancient language of Roman origin. Most people in the hospitality industry speak English.

The government is a Confederation of twenty-three Cantons that have their own government and administration. The Federal Government is responsible for defence, foreign affairs, and transport and postal systems.

Climate

Average temperatures for Zurich are: Jan max 2C, min -3C; July max 25C, min 14C. July and August are the peak tourist months, when it is necessary to queue for every attraction and service, but June and September have roughly the same weather, less crowds, and cheaper hotel tariffs.

Entry Regulations

Visitors must have a valid passport, but a visa is not required for visits up to 90 days.

The duty free allowance is 200 cigarettes or 50 cigars or 250 gm pipe tobacco; alcoholic beverages up to 15% proof 2 litres, over 15% proof 1 litre; perfumery 0.5 litre, films unrestricted if for personal use. There is no restriction on the import or export of currency. No vaccinations are required.

Currency

The currency of the land is the Swiss Franc (SFr), which is divided into 100 centimes or rappen. Approximate exchange rates, which should be used as a guide only, are:

A$	=	0.95SFr
Can$	=	1.13SFr
NZ$	=	0.77SFr
S$	=	1.00SFr
UK£	=	2.52SFr
US$	=	1.66SFr
Euro	=	1.55SFr

Notes are in denominations of 1000, 500, 100, 50, 20 and 10 Swiss Francs, and coins are 5, 2 and 1 Franc and 50, 20, 10 and 5 centimes.

Banks are ⊙open Mon-Fri 8.30am-noon, 2-4.30pm. There are no currency restrictions and at exchange offices (Bureaux de Change or Geldwechsel) most currencies can be bought or sold.

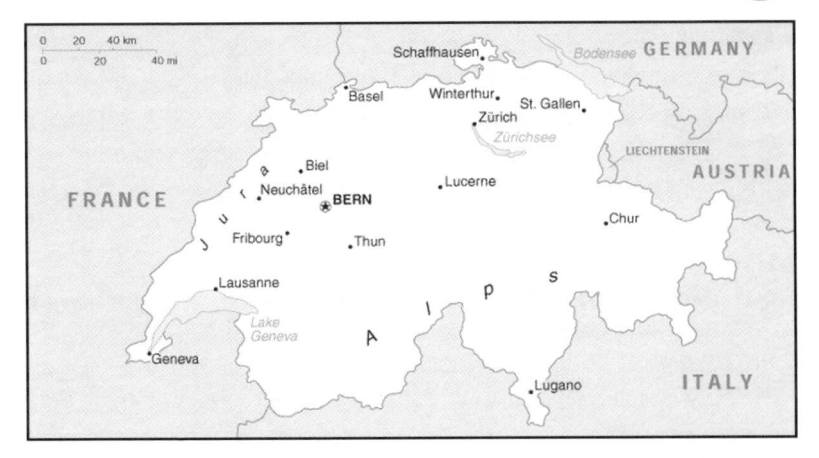

Shopping hours are ⊙Mon-Fri 8am-12.30pm, 1.30-6.30pm, Sat 8am-12.30pm, 1.30-4pm, although in the big cities the shops tend to stay open at lunchtime.

Post offices are ⊙open Mon-Fri 7.30am-noon, 1.45-6pm, Sat 8.30-11am.

Credit cards are widely accepted, though it is better to have some cash when travelling through the smaller towns. There is a Goods and Services Tax (MWST) of 6% on most items.

Telephone

International direct dialling is available and the International code is 00, the country code 41.

It is expensive to make international calls from hotels.

Driving

It is necessary to have an international driving licence to hire a car. Driving is on the right. In this country traffic coming from the right has priority, as have trams in the cities and post-buses on mountain roads.

Speed limits are:

> Motorways - 130km/h
> Open roads - 100km/h
> Built-up areas - 50km/h

On-the-spot fines can be imposed for speeding.

Miscellaneous

Local time is GMT + 1 (Central European Time). Daylight saving operates from late March to late September.

Electricity is 220v AC, with round, two-pin plugs.

Health - Switzerland has an excellent health system, but it is wise to have insurance cover.

Lucerne

Lucerne (Luzern) is the scenic capital of Central Switzerland (Zentralschweiz), which is the most-visited region of the country. Consequently there is no shortage of hotels and restaurants in this part of the world, and getting to Lucerne by road or rail is easy and picturesque.

The city is attractively situated on the banks of the Reuss River as it begins its journey from the Vierwaldstattersee (also called Lake Lucerne).

History

Central Switzerland, in particular the areas around Vierwaldstattersee, is William Tell country. This legendary national hero leapt into the lake from the wicked Gessler's boat and escaped. His story has been told in drama and music, and even if he did not actually exist, as historians believe, the events taking place in the story did.

The Rutli meadow, on the western shores of the lake, is where representatives of the Confederates of Schwyz, Uri and Unterwald met in 1291 to compose the Oath of Eternal Alliance, which formed the world's oldest still-existing democracy.

Tourist Information

The Tourist Board Luzern has its office at Bahnhofstrasse 3, ✆(41) 227 1717, fax 227 1718, and is ⊙open Mon-Fri 8am-noon 2-5.30pm, closed Sat-Sun.

A Tourist Information Centre is found at Zentralstrasse 5 (in the train station/West building), ✆(41) 227 1717, fax 227 1720. The centre is ⊙open Mon-Fri 8.30am-7.30pm, Sat-Sun 9am-7.30pm (summer); Mon-Fri 8.30am-8.30pm, Sat-Sun 9am-8.30pm (June 16-Sept 15); Mon-Fri 8.30am-6pm, Sat 9am-6pm, Sun 9am-1pm (winter).

Local Transport

There are efficient bus and trolley bus services.

Accommodation

Following is a selection of accommodation with prices for a double room per night, which should be used as a guide only.

Chateau Gutsch

Kanonenstrasse, Lucerne, ✆(041) 249 4100, fax (041) 249 4191 (✎travelweb@hotelbook.com(00913)). Built as a hotel in 1888, but you could be forgiven for thinking that it was originally a castle. 31 rooms, restaurant, bar/lounge - ✪Sfr250-450 including breakfast.

Wilden Mann Romantik Hotel, Bahnhofstrasse 30, Lucerne, ✆(041) 210 1666, fax 210 1629 (✎travelweb@hotelbook.com(00271)). 43

rooms situated in the Old Town, its facilities include 2 restaurants and a bar/lounge - ✪SFr155-420.

Grand Hotel Europe, Haldenstrasse 59, Lucerne, ✆(041) 370 0011, fax 370 1031 (✉grand-hotel-europe@bluewin.ch). Within walking distance of the town and the lake. 178 rooms, restaurant, bar/lounge - ✪SFr160-270.

Art Deco Hotel Montana, Adligenswilerstrasse 22, Lucerne, ✆(041) 410 6565, fax 410 6676 (✉travelweb@hotelbook.com(01894)). Situated 1 km from city centre with wonderful views over the Lake. Take a cable car from the lake shores to the lobby. 65 rooms, restaurant, bar/lounge - ✪SFr135-440.

Johanniter TOP Hotel, Bundesplatz 18, Lucerne, ✆(041) 231 8555, fax 210 1650 (✉travelweb@hotelbook.com(00614)). Situated 3 minutes from the railway station. Has 65 rooms, coffee lounge, bar/lounge - ✪SFr99-240.

Food and Drink

The specialty of Lucerne is *Kugelipaschtetli*, puff-pastry filled with chicken, veal or sweetbreads, mushrooms and cream sauce. Fish is also prominent on the city's menus, usually sauteed and served with tomato, mushroom and caper sauce.

Restaurants around here are not cheap, although the food is very good and so you often feel the price is justified. Here are a few at the lower end of the price scale.

Zur Pfistern, Kornmarkt 4 -a 14th century guildhall on the old-town waterfront -fish dishes are recommended - credit cards accepted.

Rebstock/Hofstube, St Leodegarstrasse 3 (next to the Hofkirche) - international cuisine in brasserie and the more formal restaurant, reservations necessary, credit cards accepted.

Galliker, Schutzenstrasse 1. Real traditional Luzerner cuisine. Popular with locals and visitors. Reservations are a good idea. Credit cards accepted. Note: this restaurant is ☉closed on Sunday and Monday from mid-July to mid-August.

Shopping

Lucerne is the main shopping venue for the entire region, so the shops tend to remain open longer than in other cities.

The main department store is ***Jelmoli***, Pilatusstrasse 4; and the chain stores are **Nordmann**, Weggisgasse 5, and ***EPA***, Rossligasse 20.

Lucerne was once a major producer of lace and embroidery goods, but although this is no longer the case, it is still one of the best places to buy Swiss handiwork. Watches are also high on people's shopping lists.

For lace and embroidered goods try:

Sturzenegger, Schwanenplatz 7.

Schmid-Linder, Denkmalstrasse 9.

Innerschweizer Heimatwerk, Franziskanerplatz 14.

For watches try:

Bucherer, Schwanenplatz, who represent Piaget and Rolex; and ***Gubelin***, Schweizerhofquai, who represent Philippe, Patek, and Audemars Piguet as well as its own brand.

Sightseeing

A walking tour can begin at the **Altes Rathaus** (Old Town Hall) which was built in the late Renaissance style between 1599 and 1606, and has been used by the town council for its meetings since 1606. It is on Rathausquai, facing the modern bridge, **Rathaus-Steg**.

On the right of the Town Hall, in Furrengasse, is the **Am Rhyn Haus**, which has a good collection of Picasso paintings from his late period. It is ☼open daily 10am-6pm (Jan-Oct); 11am-1pm, 2-4pm (Nov-Mar).

Take the stairs on the right, and pass the Zunfthaus zu Pfistern, a guildhall and restaurant, to the Kornmarkt. Cross the square and go to the left into the **Weinmarkt**, the most picturesque of the city's squares. During the 15th, 16th and 17th centuries people came from all over Europe to see the famous passion plays presented in this square, which before that time was the site of the wine market. The fountain in the centre portrays St Mauritius, the patron saint of warriors.

Now walk towards the **Spreuerbrucke**, the narrow wooden bridge that runs off Muhlenplatz. The bridge dates from 1408 and its inside gables have a series of 17th century paintings by Kaspar Meglinger of the *Dance of Death*. They are well preserved, but certainly not to everyone's taste.

The other end of the bridge brings you to the **Natur-Museum** and next to it the **Historisches Museum**. The Natural History Museum has very modern exhibits and even some live animals. It is in Kasernenplatz, and is ☼open Tues-Sat 10-noon, 2-5pm; Sun 10am-5pm. The Historical Museum, in Pfistergasse, is not really very interesting to anyone who is not Swiss, but nevertheless it is ☼open Tues-Fri 10am-noon, 2-5pm; Sat-Sun 10am-5pm.

Continue along Pfistergasse in the direction of the lake until you get to Bahnhofstrasse, turn left, then right into Munzgasse. Continue on to Franziskanerplatz and the **Franziskanerkirche** (Franciscan Church), which is more than 700 years old although it has been renovated more than a few times and lost a lot of its original style.

Go back to Bahnhofstrasse, turn right and walk past the Government Building (**Regierungsgebaude**), the home of the cantonal government, to the **Jesuitenkirche** (Jesuit Church). This church was built between 1667 and 1678, and is worth a visit. The enormous interior has been completely restored and it is a brilliant example of the Rococo style. Next door, in Theaterstrasse, is the **Stadttheater** (City Theatre). On the waterfront there is a fish market every Friday morning.

Next we cross the 14th century **Kapellbrucke** (Chapel Bridge), the oldest wooden bridge in Europe. Bridges usually go across rivers in a straight line, but not this one - it crosses diagonally. This is because it originally was a division between the river and the lake. The bridge is the symbol of Lucerne - its stone water tower, its shingled roof and its shape making it instantly recognizable, much as the Golden Gate to San Francisco and the Harbour Bridge to Sydney.

When you walk across you will notice the gables painted by Heinrich Wagman in the 17th century, but some will be empty. There were 112 panels depicting local history, legends and coats of arms, but during a fire in 1993, 78 of the paintings were completely destroyed, and some others are being carefully restored and will be replaced. The bill for rebuilding and restoring the bridge came to around 3 million Swiss francs.

From the bridge, veer towards your right through the Schwanenplatz and along Schweizerhofquai, passing the *Hotel Schweizerhof*, which has had as guests Napoleon III, Mark Twain, Leo Tolstoy and Richard Wagner.

Continue to Zurichstrasse, turn left and continue to Lowenplatz where you can't miss the **Bourbaki-Panorama**. A conical structure built as a tourist attraction and nothing else, it has a panoramic painting of the French Army retreating into Switzerland during the Franco-Prussian War. As you walk around, the painting seems to become 3-D with things coming out towards to you. There is also a recorded commentary in several languages and the whole complex is ☺open daily 9am-6pm (May-Sept), 9am-5pm (March-April and October).

The well-known restaurant, the **Old Swiss House**, is next door to the Panorama, but check out the prices before you wander in.

Lowendenkmal

From Lowenplatz take Denkmalstrasse to the **Lowendenkmal** (Lion Monument), another symbol of Lucerne that should not be missed under any circumstances. It is carved out of a sheer sandstone face and is of a dying lion, with a broken spear in his side and his chin sagging on his shield. Carved by Lucas Ahorn of Konstanz, from a design by Danish sculptor Berthel Thorwaldsen, it commemorates 760 Swiss guards, and their officers, who were killed defending Louis XVI at Tuileries in Paris in 1792. There is a Latin inscription that translates: "To the bravery and fidelity of the Swiss". When you are there, standing near the pond in front of the monument, take a moment to look at people around you. Many will have tears in their eyes, not because they feel any affinity with some brave men who died over two hundred years ago, but simply because of the spirit evoked by the carving itself.

Next to the park that houses the Lion is the **Gletschergarten** (Glacier Garden), where excavations between 1872 and 1875 revealed bedrock that had been polished and pocked by glaciers during the Ice Age. A small museum on site has impressive relief maps of Switzerland, but admission times vary dramatically so ask at the Tourist Information Office for current times.

To get back to the city centre, return to Lowenplatz, get back onto Zurichstrasse, then turn right onto Museggstrasse and follow it all the way. It actually goes through one of the 15th century city gates, and gives some good views of the old town.

The Best of Lucerne in Brief

Old City. Bordered by mountains and the lake, this medieval district boasts attractive squares including the Kornmarkt, Weinmarkt and the Hirschenplatz. There are many beautiful buildings such as the Town Hall and Pfistern guildhall.

Dying Lion Monument. This famous monument was carved to commemorate the valiant efforts of Swiss mercenaries who died protecting French royalty in Tuileries in 1792. Mark Twain described the evocative work as the "saddest and most moving piece of rock in the world".

Glacier Garden. This prehistoric garden preserves and displays blocks of ice that are remnants of the Ice Age, 15,000 to 20,000 years ago, and fossils which are more than 20 million years old.

Chapel Bridge. The Water Tower attached to the bridge, with its distinct octagonal shape, has become the city's landmark. The bridge itself was built in the fourteenth century and contains paintings depicting episodes from Lucerne's history.

Wasserturm and Kapellbrucke. These structures are remants of the town's original fortifications and date back to the fourteenth century. They are the country's landmarks, said to be its most photographed subjects.

Picasso Museum. Kept in an old and picturesque historical building, Am-Rhyn-House, are a collection of Picasso's late works, created in the 20 years leading up to his death. The gallery of 200 photographs capturing the artist is a welcome complement to his featured works.

Swiss Museum of Transport. Planes, trains and automobiles feature in Europe's most comprehensive transport museum. The history and development of different modes of travel and also of communication technology is expounded with the use of hundreds of visual exhibits. There are many old vehicles and other nostalgic memorabilia.

The Jesuit Church. A great Baroque building, this church was built by Father Vogler in the seventeenth century and was the first of its architectural kind in the country.

Town Hall. An attractive seventeenth century building constructed in the Italian Renaissance style.

Zurich

The largest city in Switzerland, Zurich has a population of around 400,000 and is situated on the Limmat River and along the shores of the northern tip of the Zurichsee (*see* = lake).

Zurich is a very beautiful city, and a commercial, industrial and university centre. One could be forgiven for wondering why it is not the capital of Switzerland, but that honour goes to Bern.

History

It is known that the area was inhabited as early as 4500BC, for land and marine archaeologists have discovered artifacts from many Stone Age and Iron Age settlements around the lake.

The Romans, ever on the lookout for a good, central location, built a customs house on a hill overlooking the river in the 1st century BC. The customs house became a fortress, and remains of it can still be seen. Legend has it that the Romans were also responsible for providing Zurich with its patron saints. During the Roman occupation, the Roman governor beheaded a brother and sister, Felix and Regula, because they were Christians. That part is historically correct, but the rest has yet to be proven. After their execution they picked up their heads, waded through the water, and marched up a hill before succumbing at a spot where the Grossmunster now stands.

The Romans were ousted in the 5th century by the ancestors of the present occupants, but the importance of the town dwindled until four hundred years later when the Carolingians built an imperial palace on the banks of the Limmat. Then Louis the German, grandson of Charlemagne, had an abbey built where the Fraumunster now stands.

Zurich's flair for trade and commerce was evident by the 12th century, and the merchants became very powerful. This was not appreciated by the tradesmen and labourers who, led by an aristocrat named Rudolf Brun, took the merchants on, and defeated the town council. They then established the guilds for which Zurich is famous, and in fact the original thirteen guilds retained their power until the French Revolution. They still have their prestige, shown by the annual festival when businessmen don medieval costumes for the procession through the city to the guildhalls.

During the Reformation, a leader named Huldrych Zwingli preached in the Grossmunster, exhorting the populace to thrift and hard work. His success can be measured by the fact that the Zurich stock exchange is the fourth most important in the world (after New York, London and Tokyo) and turns over on average 636 billion Swiss Francs each year.

Tourist Information

The tourist information office is in the Main Railway Station, ✆(01) 215 4000, fax 215 4099, and it is ⏰open Mon-Fri 8.30am-9.30pm,

Sat-Sun 8.30am-8.30pm (April-October; Mon-Fri 8.30am-7.30pm, Sat-Sun 8.30am-6.30pm (November-March). (✆www.zurichtourism.ch)

Local Transport

Zurich has a very efficient tram service from 5.15am to midnight. Tickets must be purchased from vending machines before boarding.

Taxis are not really an alternative as they are very expensive - ✪10SFr minimum.

Accommodation

Following is a selection of accommodation with prices for a double room per night, which should be used as a guide only.

Arabella Sheraton Atlantis Hotel, Doeltschiweg 234, Zurich, ✆(01) 454 5454, fax 454 5400. Set in forested parkland 10 minutes from the city centre. 2 restaurants, bar/lounges - standard room ✪SFr270-395, deluxe room SFr325-475.

Hotel Schweizerhof, Bahnhof Platz 7, Zurich, ✆(01) 218 8888, fax 218 8181. Centrally located Superior First Class hotel. 147 rooms, restaurant, cafe, bar/lounge - ✪SFr270-490.

Arabella Sheraton Neues Schloss, Stockerstrasse 17, ✆(01) 286 9400, fax 286 9445. Situated in the business district. 58 rooms, restaurant, bar/lounge - standard room ✪SFr240-380, deluxe room SFr264-410.

Rigihof TOP Hotel, Universitatstrasse 101, Zurich, ✆(01) 361 1685, fax 361 1617 (✉travelweb@hotelbook.com(00620)). Only 1km from the city centre. 65 rooms, restaurant, bar/lounge - ✪SFr200-270.

Zurich's **Youth Hostel** is **Wollishofen**, Mutschellenstrasse 114, ✆(01) 482 3544, fax (01) 481 9992.

Food and Drink

A few dishes spring to mind when thinking of Switzerland - cheese fondue, rosti and veal in cream and white wine sauce. Everyone knows of the first and last, but *rosti* might be new to some. It is a cake of hash-brown potatoes crisped in a skillet and flavoured with bacon, herbs or cheese. Delicious.

The Swiss use a lot of cheese in their main courses, and a lot of chocolate in their desserts. Speaking of chocolate, it is available everywhere and is simply the best, though it is not cheap. Actually, eating anything in Switzerland, and in Zurich particularly, is an expensive exercise. Probably the best bet is to have the main meal at lunch-time and take advantage of the reduced prices for business lunches. Here are a few restaurants that won't charge an arm and leg:

Zeughauskeller, Bahnhofstrasse 23, ✆(01) 211 2690 - 15th century building that is popular with locals and visitors alike - reservations necessary for lunch - no credit cards accepted.

Mere Catherine, Nagelihof 3, ✆(01) 262 2250 - bistro with a varied menu and an interesting clientele - no credit cards accepted.

Rheinfelder Bierhaus, Marktgasse 19, ✆(01) 251 2991 - somewhat dreary decor but excellent home-made meals. They do not accept credit cards.

Shopping

The main department stores are **Jelmoli**, Bahnhofstrasse at Seidengasse, ✆(01) 220 4411, and **Globus**, Bahnhofstrasse at Lowenplatz, ✆(01) 221 3311. Smaller chain stores are **Vilan**, Bahnhofstrasse 75, ✆229 5111 and **ABM**, Bellevueplatz, ✆261 4484.

The main shopping street, as you may have worked out for yourself, is **Bahnhofstrasse** and the Paradeplatz end, towards the lake, has the more exclusive shops and boutiques.

A **flea market** is held ☉every Saturday 6am-3.30pm at Burkliplatz, which is at the lake end of Bahnhofstrasse.

Sightseeing

The main sights of Zurich are easily seen on a walking tour and the best place to begin is the **Hauptbahnhof** (Main Railway Station). When the enormous station was first built, in the 1800s, it was considered to be a work of beauty. Time has taken its toll. The current restoration program has been going on for some time. It is expected to be even grander than before.

The **Schweizerisches Landesmuseum** (Swiss National Museum) is at Museumstrasse 2, behind the station, in a huge Gothic building. Exhibits include Stone Age objects, early watches, dress and furniture from earlier times, and models of military battles. A mural by Ferdinand Hodler entitled *Retreat of the Swiss Confederates at Marignano* is in the Hall of Arms. The museum is ☉open Tues-Sun 10am-5pm and admission is free.

The statue in the centre of Bahnhofplatz is of **Alfred Escher**, a financial wizard and politician who was responsible for Zurich becoming a major banking centre. He was also involved in the development of the city's university, the Federal Railways and the tunnel under the St Gotthard Pass.

There is a subterranean passage under Bahnhofplatz that comes out at **Bahnhofstrasse**, the city's main street and principal shopping strip.

Continue along this street until you come to Rennweg, on the left. Turn into it and then left again onto Fortunagasse, then continue on to the **Lindenhof Square**. Here there are remains of the Roman fortress and a medieval imperial residence. There is also a fountain that commemorates the women of Zurich who, in 1292, saved the town from the Habsburgs. Apparently the town was all but defeated when the women donned uniforms and armour and marched to the Lindenhof. When the enemy saw them coming they assumed that it was a second, fresh army and so fled the scene.

A short walk from here to your right takes you to the St Peterhof and **St Peterskirche**, the oldest parish church in Zurich. There has been a church on this site since the 9th century, but the present building dates only from the 13th century. In the tower is the largest clock face in Europe. Again walking to your right, turn into Schlusselgasse, then into an alley named Thermengasse. Through grates you will be able to see beneath you the ruins of **Roman baths**, which have been excavated. There are signs giving details of the dig. Continue on to **Weinplatz** which has some excellent shops, and opens onto the riverside. After checking out the shops, continue on your way, crossing the Rathaus Bridge over the river.

The street that runs along the riverbank on this side is called **Limmat Quai** and near here at nos. 40, 42 and 54 there are some interesting guildhalls (*zunfthausen*) that are now restaurants. No. 40 is **Zunfthaus zur Zimmerleuten** which dates from 1708 and was for carpenters; no. 42 is **Gesellschaftshaus zum Ruden** a 13th century noblemen's hall; and no. 54 is **Zunfthaus zur Saffran** a 14th century haberdashers' meeting place.

Across from no. 54 is the 17th century Baroque **Rathaus** (Town Hall), which can only be visited by people attending the cantonal Parliament Monday morning meeting, or the city Parliament Wednesday afternoon meeting. The interior is in good condition and the stucco ceiling in the Banquet Hall is worth a look.

Further along Limmat Quai is the 15th century **Wasserkirche** (Water Church) built in the late-Gothic style with stained glass by Giacometti. Attached to the church is the **Helmhaus** which dates from the 18th century. Here a linen market was once held, but now it has changing contemporary art exhibitions. It is ◉open Tues-Sun 10am-6pm (until 9pm Thurs), and for more information ✆251 7166. Both these buildings were once on an island, the one where Felix and Regula lost their heads.

Continuing towards the lake the next stop is the very grand **Grossmunster**. The church was built on the site of a Carolingian church which was dedicated to Felix and Regula, as this was as far as they carried their heads, and where they were buried. Legend has it that Charlemagne decided that a church should be built on the spot when his horse stumbled over their graves. There is a huge statue of Charlemagne near the south tower, but it is only a copy - the original is in the crypt for safe-keeping. The inside of the church is very austere, but remember that this was where Zwingli preached his 'thrift and hard work' sermons.

Follow Limmat Quai to Ramistrasse, and if you are interested in art, turn left and continue on to the **Kunsthaus** (Art Gallery) on Heimplatz. It is ✪open Tues-Thurs 10am-9pm, Sat-Sun 10am-5pm, ✆251 6755. Also on Heimplatz is the **Schauspielhaus** (Theatre), which was the only German-language theatre in the world that was not controlled from Berlin during the Second World War.

If you are not interested in art, turn right onto Ramistrasse, and on Bellevueplatz is the **Opern Haus** (Opera House), built in 1890 and renovated between 1980 and 1984.

As you continue across **Quai Brucke** (Bridge) take time to notice the great views both to the right of the city, and to the left of the lake. The views are particularly good at night, so a return visit is a good idea.

At the end of the bridge veer to the right, then take the second street on the right, Fraumunsterstrasse, which leads, of course, to the **Fraumunster**. Built on the site of a 9th century abbey, whose remains can be seen, the Fraumunster was originally Gothic in style, then in 1732 the beautiful narrow spires were added. The Romanesque choir has stained-glass windows by Marc Chagall.

At Munsterhof 20 is the Baroque **Zunfthaus zur Meisen**, an 18th century guildhall for the wine merchants that now houses the

Landesmuseum's ceramics collection, ⓒ221 2144. ⊕Open Tues-Fri and Sun 10am-noon, 2-5pm, Sat 10am-noon, 2-4pm. Also in this square is the **Zunfthaus zur Waag**, a 17th century guildhall for the linen weavers and hat makers.

Walk along Poststrasse to Paradeplatz, a major crossroads and centre on Bahnhofstrasse, from where you can catch a train back to the railway station, or wherever you are staying.

The Best of Zurich in Brief

Grossmunster. This is the city's most famous landmark - its distinct dual towers are responsible for establishing this honour. The building now functions as part of the University, appropriately containing the theological faculty. Romanesque architecture can be identified in the cloisters, which were built in the twelfth century. Sculptures from this period are housed inside.

Fraumunster. The highlight of this church is the stained glass windows, added in 1970 at the hands of Chagall. The church foundations are thought to date back to the ninth century A.D.

Lindenhof. Preserved from Roman times, this area contains a Roman tombstone, customs post and small fort. There are great views from its elevated position.

Zunfthaus zum Meisen. Porcelain displays and the rococo interior decoration make this wonderful 18th century Baroque building worth visiting.

St. Peter's Church. St. Peter's is the city's oldest church and bears Europe's largest clock face, spanning 8.7 metres.

Tonhalle. This superb concert hall, renowned for its fine acoustics, plays host to the talents of the Zurich Chamber

Orchestra and the Tonhalle Orchestra. It is more than a century old. *Gotthardstrasse 5*.

Schauspielhaus. This is Zurich's largest and most famous theater. It became something of a sanctuary during WWII, frequented by such talents as Bertolt Brecht. *Raemistrasse 34*.

Opera House. World-class performances are on show for most of the year and include symphonies, ballets and, naturally, operas, all covering a refreshing array of different styles. The auditorium is crafted in a wonderful Neo-baroque style. *Falkenstrasse 1*.

Swiss National Museum. Traces the interesting history of Switzerland and exhibits many pieces of national interest.

Niederdorff. When the sun drops, locals and tourists flock to Niederdorff to become part of the vibrant nightlife.

Kunsthaus. Modern and nineteenth century art in various forms is displayed in the city's top gallery. *Heimplatz*.

Bahnhofstrasse. The place to shop, or at least to window shop. This retail stretch is popular and picturesque.

Museum Rietberg. For something different, this museum contains interesting exhibits from Asia and the African continent.

Urania Observatory. The tower at this observatory stands almost 50 metres high and the complex has a bar with superb views over the city below.

Bern

Bern, the capital of Switzerland, is nestled into a bend of the Aare River in the country's mid-west. This attractive city, by no means Switzerland's largest with a population of only 140,000, has the appeal of its well preserved medieval Altstadt and its function as a gateway to the wonderful Bernese Oberland to the south.

Einstein's house is here, and the genius occupied it while developing some of his most famous theories. It is not really worth the trip to see, however, unless you are a physics fanatic or hope to find a secret brain tonic hidden away in a forgotten cupboard.

Bern is not a city of must-see sights. Its allure lies in its general charm and the quality of its Old Town. If you're in Bern, make sure it's because you're on your way to the Swiss Alps, and don't spend too much time here. Any more than a day is time that could have been better spent up in the glorious alpine mountains.

Tourist Information

Bern Tourism is at the main train station, Bahnhof, ✆(31) 328 1212. It is ⏰open 9am-6pm on weekdays with reduced hours on Sunday and extra hours in the evenings between June and September. Enquire here about organised city tours.

Accommodation

Prices given are for a double room per night and should be used as a guide only.

Hotel Schweizerhof, Bahnhofplatz 11, ✆326 8080, fax 326 8090. One of the best hotels in Bern, the Schweizerhof has been in operation since 1859, and run by the same family. The five star boutique hotel is sumptuously decorated, has its own private art collection, boasts wonderful service and is in an excellent location. There are 84 welcoming rooms, many of which were renovated a few years ago and

Bern on a misty morning

had air-conditioning installed. Everything is placed at your fingertips - ✪Sfr345-420.

Hotel Alfa, Laupenstrasse 15, ✆388 0111, fax 388 0110. A three star hotel offering 52 well equipped rooms with a modern look and feel. It is great for access to public transport, only three minutes walk from the main railway station, and is situated on the fringe of the Altstadt - ✪Sfr196 including buffet breakfast.

Hotel Mövenpick Wächter, Neuengasse 44, ✆321 15 21, fax 321 1516, ✉hotel.waechter@moevenpick.com. 42 comfortable, well appointed rooms and two restaurants ensure you are well looked after. The hotel is situated conveniently next to the Bahnhof - ✪Sfr158.

Best of Bern In Brief

Old Town (Altstadt). Many charming buildings grace these streets. Make this walk a top priority and spend at least a couple of hours getting to know the heart of Bern.

Clock Tower (Zeitglocken). Mechanical figures pop out of this sixteenth century monument to entertain the crowds below.

Bear Pits (Barengraben). These city mascots are well tended by keepers in their habitat on the other side of the Aare River. Visitors come to see them, as they have done in a tradition stretching back more than 500 years. *Grosser Muristalden.*

Museum of Fine Arts (Kunstmuseum). The extensive collection of Paul Klee paintings are the main feature here. *Hodlerstrasse 12.*

Cathedral of St Vincent (Munster). Great views over Bern can be enjoyed from the tower top of this fifteenth century gothic church. *Munsterplatz.*

Geneva

Geneva is most noted for its banking industry, the headquarters of world organisations including the United Nations (European division) and the Red Cross, and its picturesque setting on Lake Geneva.

If you trip over something on a city street, bend down to make sure it is not a wallet overflowing with a wad of 1000Sfr bank notes. Money floods through this city, and you can see it everywhere in the form of immaculate cars and impeccable suits.

Geneva is primarily a business centre, and there are better places in Switzerland for tourists to visit, but if you find yourself here there are a few sights worth seeing.

Tourist Information

Tourist Information can be obtained from the office at 18 rue du Mont Blanc, ✆909 7000. They are ⏰open 9am-8pm on weekdays and all day on weekends, with slightly shorter hours in the winter months. The telephone area code is 22.

Accommodation

Hotel Mon-Repos, 131-133, Rue de Lausanne, ✆909 3 909, fax 909 39 93, ✉clients@hmrge.ch. Overlooking Lake Geneva and fine city parklands, and neighbouring the buildings of international organisations, this hotel is geared toward the business traveller, but comfortable facilities ensure tourists will also enjoy an adequate stay at good value. The hotel has 80 rooms on six floors - ✪Sfr133.

Hotel Les Arcades, Place Cornavin 14/16, ✆732 59 48, fax 738 39 46, ✉hotel_arcades@hotmail.com. Rooms have standard facilities but the soundproofed windows will ensure that you at least get a quiet night's rest - ✪Sfr135 including breakfast and tax.

Best of Geneva In Brief

Flower Clock. This attractive florally-decorated timepiece is worth the stroll to see. Nearby, out in Lake Geneva, you will notice the jet-propelled spray of the water fountain. *Jardin Anglais*.

International Red Cross Museum. Guides visitors through the history of the Red Cross, from the organisation's inception in 1863 through its involvement in the some of the worst battlefields and humanitarian crises in modern history. *Avenue de la Paix 17*.

Petite Palais. This gallery showcases the works of a selection of famous artists, including Cezanne and Picasso. *Terrasse St-Victor 2*.

Chateau Chillon. Consider taking a day trip from Geneva to this beautiful thirteenth century castle on the eastern side of Lake Geneva near Montreux. Take your time exploring every nook and cranny of the photogenic sight, then relax on the banks of the lake for the afternoon before your one hour return rail trip.

View of the left entrance, Chateau Chillon

View from the keep rooftop, Chateau Chillon

Interlaken

Only 40 minutes from Bern by train, Interlaken is surrounded by the wonderful white landscapes of its neighbouring Alps. It is overrun by backpackers and haunted by the lingering memory of 21 canyoning adventurers, including 14 Australians, who where tragically swept away by flash floods in 1999.

Interlaken is best used as a base for a trip to the stunning Jungfrau mountain. If you are here in winter, take advantage of the skiing opportunities on the surrounding slopes, or in nearby Grindelwald.

Tourist Information

The information office, Hoheweg 37, ✆822 2121, is ⊙open all day on weekdays and for half the day on Saturdays during the peak summer season (July-August), and in the mornings until midday for the remainder of the year. They can assist you with accommodation enquiries, and there are hotels and budget establishments in Interlaken to meet the needs of every traveller.

Best of Interlaken In Brief

Walking. Enjoy the fresh air, take in the extensive parklands and admire the Gothic architecture. This is best way to explore Interlaken.

Activities. The information office will provide details of available adventure sports, which have become a burgeoning industry in the area. But be warned that the most extreme of these are dangerous and extra care should be taken.

Jungfrau. Although it involves a very expensive rail trip, a visit to Jungfrau is an absolute must. Be consoled that you are on your way to the highest railway station in Europe, and that the feeling of standing on top of the world is just reward. Highlights - apart from the panoramic views, of course - are the Ice Palace and Sphinx Tunnel.

Driving Through Switzerland

A Scenic Tour of Switzerland by Road

Itinerary - 8 Days - Distance 666kms

Geneva is the second city in Switzerland, and is situated at the western end of Lake Geneva. This city is the European headquarters of the United Nations, and of the Red Cross. The old part of the city has buildings dating from the 12th century. From Geneva head north along the shores of Lake Geneva through **Nyon** and **Morges**, little towns on the shores of the lake. From here you reach **Lausanne**, a university town on the northern shore of Lake Geneva. Lausanne is the headquarters of the International Olympic Committee, and houses an interesting Olympic museum.

Drive north towards Neuchatel Lake. **Yverdon** is a spa and resort town at the southern end of the lake. The town of **Neuchatel** is very picturesque. From here, drive through **Biel/Bienne**, a tourist town, with many interesting old buildings. Close by is **Bern**, the capital of the Swiss confederation of states. The Parliament Buildings are here, as is the famous Bear Pit. There are many historic buildings here.

From Berne drive east towards **Lucerne**. Lucerne is a very scenic town on the shores of Lake Lucerne, with buildings dating from Gothic and Renaissance times. Head south from Lucerne to **Altdorf** through a mountain tunnel. At Altdorf you can see the William Tell Memorial and museum. Further south you drive through some scenic but mountainous roads to **Brig**. This town is the starting point for travel to Zermatt and the Matterhorn. To reach Zermatt you can leave your car in the car park, and take the mountain railway up to the town.

From the town of **Sion** you can see the tallest dam in the world on Grand Dixience Lake. Head back to **Montreux** through little villages, all popular for winter sports, such as skiing. Montreux is on the eastern end of Lake Geneva and is famous for its music festivals.

Continue back to Geneva along the southern shores of the lake (through France) through the resort towns of **Evian** and **Thonon**.

PART THREE

Index

A

Academy of Fine Arts, 97
Accommodation and Eating Out, 9-10
Alberg, 107
Albertina, 93
Alfred Escher, 124
Alpirsbach, 81
Altdorf, 135
Alte Hofburg, 92
Alte Pinakothek, 76
Alter Hof, 74
Alter Markt, 58, 100
Altes Rathaus, 115
Am Rhyn Haus, 116
American Express, 13, 32
Antikenmuseum, 46
Anton-Neumayr Platz, 101
Art Institute, 65
Asamkirche, 74

Augustinian Church, 95
Ausserfern, 107
Austria, 83-108
   Climate, 83
   Currency, 85
   Driving, 86
   Entry Regulations, 84-85
   Miscellaneous, 86-87
   Shopping, 85
   Telephone, 86
Austrian National Tourist Office, 24

B

Bad Durkheim, 79
Bad Godesberg, 53
Bad Hogastein, 108
Bad Ischl, 108
Baden-Baden, 78, 81
Badgastein, 108
Bahnhof Zoo, 44
Bahnhofstrasse, 124, 128

banks, 36, 85, 110
Bavarian National Museum, 76
Bear Pits, 131
Beethovenhaus, 53, 54
Belvedere, 45
Belvedere Palace, 94
Berlin, 7, 38-51, 82
   Accommodation, 41
   Best of Berlin in Brief, 50-51
   Food and Drink, 42
   History, 39
   Local Transport, 40
   Outside Berlin, 48-50
   Shopping, 42-43
   Sightseeing, 43-48
   Tourist Information, 39
Berlin Zoo, 50
Bern, 8, 129-131, 135
   Accommodation, 129-130

Best of Bern in Brief, 130-131
Tourist Information, 129
Biel, 135
Black Forest, 8, 78-79, 81
Best of The Black Forest in Brief, 78-79
Tourist Information, 78
BMW Museum, 77
Bodensee, 81
Bonn, 7, 52-54, 80
Best of Bonn in Brief, 54
History, 52
Sightseeing, 53-54
Tourist Information, 52
Bourbaki-Panorama, 117-118
Brandenburg, 82
Brandenburg Gate, 48
Brandenburger Tor, 47
Braubach, 80
Braunschweig, 82
Brig, 135
Brohan Museum, 46
Burg Theatre, 92
burghers' houses, 100
Burgtor, 93
Buses, 17

C

Cafe Bazar, 103
Cafe Stephanie, 75
Cafe Tomaselli, 100
Cafe Winkler, 101
Cameras and Film, 31-32
Carinthia Street, 96
Capuchin Monastery, 103
Castle, 66
Cathedral (Cologne), 57, 59
Cathedral (Salzburg), 102
Cathedral of Our Lady, 77
Cathedral of St Vincent, 131
Chapel Bridge, 119
Charlottenburg, 43

Charlottenburg Palace, 45-46, 50
Charlottenburger Tor, 47
Chateau Chillon, 132-133
Church of the Holy Trinity, 103
Church of the Immaculata, 101
Clock Tower, 131
Clothing Sizes and Conversion Chart, 31
Men's Clothing, 31
Women's Clothing, 31
Cologne, 7, 54-60
Accommodation, 56-57
Best of Cologne in Brief, 59-60
Food and Drink, 57
History, 55
Local Transport, 55
Sightseeing, 57
Tourist Information, 55
Commerzbank building, 67
Contact Details and Valuables, 13-14
credit cards, 12, 13, 36, 85, 111

D

Dachau, 76
Danube, 96
Darmstadt, 66, 79
Dessau, 82
Deutsche Guggenheim Berlin, 51
Die Bahn, 16
Driving Through Austria, 107-108
Driving Through Germany, 79-82
Germany from East to West, 81-82
The Black Forest, 81
The Rhine and Moselle Valleys, 79-81

Driving Through Germany, Austria and Switzerland, 15
Driving Through Switzerland, 134-136
Dying Lion Monument, 118, 119

E

Egyptian Museum, 46, 50
Ehrwald, 107
Eisriesenwelt, 108
electricity, 38, 86, 112
email, 32
Englischer Garten, 75, 77
Ethnological Museum (Frankfurt), 65
Ethnological Museum (Vienna), 92
Eurail, 15, 16
Europa Centre, 44, 47
Europe Online, 24
European Time Zones, 30
European Travel Commission, 24
Evian, 136
Excavations Museum, 102
exercise, 18, 19

F

Feldherrnhalle, 74
Feldkirch, 107
Festspielhaus, 101
Film, 31, 32
Flower Clock, 132
Folk Museum, 107
Franciscan Church, 101
Frankfurt am Main, 7, 60-67, 80
Accommodation, 61-63
Best of Frankfurt in Brief
Food and Drink, 63-64
Local Transport, 61
Places Further Afield, 66
Sightseeing, 64-66
Tourist Information, 61

Index

Franziskanerkirche, 116
Frauenkirche, 73
Fraumunster, 126, 127
Freiburg, 81
Friedrich Wilhelms Universitat, 53
Friedrichs-Hafen, 81
French, 28-30
   Communicating, 28-29
   Days, 29
   Numbers, 29-30
   Travel, 28
   When you get there, 28
Freudenstadt, 81

G
Gemaldegalerie, 51
Geneva, 8, 131-133, 134
   Accommodation, 132
   Best of Geneva in Brief, 132
   Tourist Information, 131
German, 25-28
   Communicating, 26-27
   Days, 27
   Numbers, 27-28
   Travel, 25-26
   When you get there, 26
German Architectural Museum, 65
German Cathedral, 51
German Film Museum, 65
German Museum of Masterpieces of Science and Technology, 76
German National Tourism Office, 24
Germany, 35-82
   Climate, 35
   Currency, 36
   Driving, 38
   Entry Regulations, 35, 36
   Miscellaneous, 38
   Telephone, 37

Gesellschaftshaus zum Ruden, 125
Getreidgasse, 104
Glacier Garden, 118, 119
Glockenspiel Tower, 102, 104
Glyptotek, 74
Gmunden, 108
Goethehaus, 64, 67
Grosser Stern, 47
Grossmunster, 126, 127
Guard House, 67
Gurzenich, 58

H
Habsburg Crypt, 93
Halle, 82
Hallein, 108
Hannover, 82
Hauptbahnhof, 124
Hauptwache, 64
Haus der Kunst, 77
Health, 18-20, 38, 86, 112
   Adjusting, 19
   Fitness, 18-19
   Medicine, 19-20
Hechingen, 81
Heidelberg, 7, 67, 68-70, 79
   Accommodation, 69
   History, 68
Helmhaus, 125
Heppenheim, 79
Historical Garden, 67
Historical Rooms, 46
Historical Museum, 67
Historisches Museum (Frankfurt), 65
Historisches Museum (Lucerne), 116
Hofbrauhaus, 74, 77
Hofburg, 107
Hofburg Palace, 95
Hofgarten, 75
Hofkirche, 107
Hohensalzburg fortress, 101-102, 105

Horse-Pond, 101
Hotel Sacher, 93

I
Idar Oberstein, 79
Imhoff-Stollwerck Chocolate Museum, 60
Imperial Cathedral, 64-65, 67
Imperial Hall, 67
Innsbruck, 8, 105-107
   Accommodation, 106
   Best of Innsbruck in Brief, 106-107
   Tourist Information, 105
Insurance, 14-15
Interlaken, 8, 133-134
   Best of Interlaken in Brief, 134
   Tourist Information, 133
International Red Cross Museum, 132
Internet Information, 10
Introduction, 11-33

J
Jenbach, 108
Jesuitenkirche, 117, 120
Judisches Gemeindehaus, 44
Jungfrau, 134

K
Kaidersaal, 64
Kaiser-Wilhelm-Gedachtniskirche, 43, 51
Kaisergruft, 96
Kapellbrucke, 117, 119
Kapuziner Church, 93
Katharinekirche, 64
Kaub, 80
Kaufhaus des Westens, 51
Keeping Up-to-Date, 33
Kitzbuhel, 108
Koblenz, 80
Kolner Philharmonie, 60

Kongresshalle, 47
Krems, 108
Kunsthaus, 126
Kurfurstendamm, 43-44, 51

L

Lahnstein, 80
Landestheater, 103
Language, 25-30
Lausanne, 134-135
Leipzig, 82
Lenbach House, 75
Liebfrauenkirche, 64
Liebighaus, 66
Limmat Quai, 125
Lindau, 81
Lindenhof Square, 124, 127
Lipizzaner Museum, 96
Looshaus, 92
Loreto Church, 103
Lowendenkmal, 118
Lucerne, 8, 112-120, 135
   Accommodation, 113-114
   Best of Lucerne in Brief, 119-120
   Food and Drink, 114-115
   History, 112-113
   Local Transport, 113
   Shopping, 115
   Sightseeing, 115-118
   Tourist Information, 113
Ludwig Museum, 60

M

Mail and Contacting Home, 32
Mainz, 80
Magdeburg, 82
Maps, 10
Maria-Therea-Strasse, 107
Maria Theresia, 93
Marienplatz, 73
Marktplatz, 53
Marionette Theatre, 103

Mastercard, 13
Mathildenhohe, 66
Mausoleum, 45
Meersburg, 81
Melk, 108
Merseburg, 82
Mirabell Gardens, 102-103, 104
Mirabell Palace, 104
Monchsberg, 101, 105
Money, 12-13
Montreux, 132, 135-136
Morges, 134
Mozart Geburthaus, 100-101
Mozart Residence, 103
Mozart's Birthplace, 103
Mozarteum, 103
Munich, 7, 70-78
   Accommodation, 71-72
   Best of Munich in Brief, 76-78
   Food and Drink, 72
   History, 70
   Local Transport, 71
   Sightseeing, 73-76
   Tourist Information, 70
Munich City Museum, 77
Munster St Martin, 53
Museum of Arts and Crafts, 65
Museum Carolino Augusteum, 105
Museum of Fine Arts (Vienna), 93, 95
Museum of Fine Arts (Bern), 131
Museum of the Wall, 50
Museum Rietberg, 128

N

Nationaltheatre, 74
National Library, 92
Natur-Museum, 116
Natural History Museum (Berlin), 51

Natural History Museum (Vienna), 93
Neuchatel, 135
Neue Hofburg, 92
Neue Pinakothek, 76
Neuhausen. 81
Neuwied, 80
New Residence, 102
New Town Hall, 73-74
Niederdorff, 128
Nymphenburg Palace, 77
Nyon, 134

O

Old Opera House, 67
Old Town (Bern), 130
Old Town (Innsbruck), 106-107
Old Town (Munich), 76
Old Town Hall, 73
Olympic Park Stadium, 78
On the Plane, 20-23
   Alcohol, 21
   Sleeping, 20-21
   Where to Sit, 21-23
Opera House (Vienna), 93, 96
Opera House (Zurich), 126, 128
Orangerie, 46
Osnabruck, 81

P

Palmengarten, 66
Parliament House (Vienna), 92
Passport, 11-12
Paulskirche, 64
Pergamon Museum, 51
Peterskirche, 74
Petite Palais, 132
Pforzheim, 81
phone cards, 32
Picasso Museum, 119
Plaster Cast House, 46-47

Index

Platz der Opfer des Nationalsozialismus, 74
post offices, 32, 36, 111
Postal Museum, 65
Potsdam, 48-50, 82
Preface, 7-10
How To Use This Book, 9-10
Propylaon, 75

Q
Quai Brucke, 126

R
Rail Pass Express, 16, 24
RailEurope, 16, 24
Rathaus-Steg, 115
Reichstag, 48
Regierungsgebaude, 116
Residence, 102
Residenz, 74, 76, 104
Residenzmuseum, 74
Residenzplatz, 102
Rheingarten, 60
Ring, The, 92
Roman baths, 125
Roman churches, 60
Roman town wall, 58
Romisch-Germanisches Museum, 58, 60
Royal Palace, 54
Rudesheim, 80

S
Salzburg, 8, 97-105, 108
  Accommodation, 99
  Best of Salzburg in Brief, 103-105
  Food and Drink, 99
  History, 97-98
  Local Transport, 98
  Sightseeing, 100-103
  Tourist Information, 98
Salzburg Cathedral, 103
Sanssouci Palace, 48-50
Schauspielhaus, 126, 128
Schloss Nymphenburg, 75
Schloss Mirabell, 103
Schluchsee, 78
Schonbrunn Palace, 94-95, 97
Schwabing, 75
Schnikel Pavilion, 45
Seefeld, 107
shopping hours, 36, 85, 111
Sigmaringen, 81
Sion, 135
Smallest House of Salzburg, 100
Sound of Music Tour, 105
Spanish Riding School, 92-93, 96
Spreuerbrucke, 116
St Anton, 107
St Florian's Fountain, 100
St Goar, 80
St Goarshausen, 80
St Margaret's Chapel, 101
St Margen, 79
St Mark's Church, 101
St Martin's Church, 58
St Michael's Church (Munich), 73, 77
St Michael's Church (Salzburg), 102
St Paul's Church, 67
St Peter, 79
St Peter's Abbey, 101
St Peter's Church (Munich), 77
St Peter's Church (Zurich), 125, 127
St Sebastian's Church, 103
St Stephen's Cathedral, 94, 96
St Wolfgang, 108
Stadt Museum, 74
State Art Gallery, 44
Stiftskirche St Peter, 103
Stock Exchange, 92
Stockerau, 108
Stuttgart, 81
Swiss Museum of Transport, 120
Swiss National Museum, 124, 128
Switzerland, 109-136
  Climate, 110
  Currency, 110-111
  Driving, 111-112
  Entry Regulations, 110
  Miscellaneous, 112
  Telephone, 111
Switzerland Tourism, 24
Symbols, 9

T
Taxes, 10, 87
Taxis, 16-17
Technical University, 47
Theatinerkirche, 74
Theseus Temple, 92
Thomas Cook, 13
Thonon, 136
Tiergarten, 50
Tierpark, 45
time, local, 38, 86, 112
Titisee, 78, 81
Tonhalle, 127
Town Hall (Bonn), 53, 54
Town Hall (Cologne), 58, 60
Town Hall (Frankfurt), 67
Town Hall (Lucerne), 120
Town Hall (Salzburg), 100
Town Hall (Vienna), 92
Town Hall (Zurich), 125
Traben-Trarbachr, 79
Trains, 15-16
Travel Agents, 23
travellers cheques, 12
Triberg, 79
Tubingen, 81

U
University, 92
Unter-Uhldingen, 81
Unter den Linden, 48

Urania Observatory, 128

V
Victory Monument, 47
Victualienmarkt, 74
Vienna, 8, 87-97, 108
   Accommodation, 88-91
   Best of Vienna in Brief, 95-97
   Food and Drink, 91-92
   History, 87-88
   Local Transport, 88
   Sights Further Afield, 94
   Sightseeing, 92-94
   Tourist Information, 88
Vienna Boys' Choir, 96
Visa, 13
Volksgarten, 92

W
Wallraf-Richartz Museum, 60
Wasserkirche, 125
Wasserturm, 119
Web Addresses, 24
Weinmarkt, 116
Weinplatz, 125
Weisbaden, 80
What To Take, 17-18
Wine Tasting, 97
Wittenberg, 82

Y
Your Accommodation, 23-24
Yverdon, 135

Z
Zell, 79
Zell Am See, 108
Zoo, 66
Zoologistche Garten, 44-45
Zunfthaus zur Meisen, 126, 127
Zunfthaus zur Saffran, 125
Zunfthaus zur Waag, 127
Zunfthaus zur Zimmerleuten, 125
Zurich, 8, 120-128
   Accommodation, 122
   Best of Zurich in Brief, 127-128
   Food and Drink, 122-123
   History, 120-121
   Local Transport, 122
   Shopping, 123
   Sightseeing, 124-127
   Tourist Information, 121-122

Travel Diary

Travel Diary

Travel Diary

147

Travel Diary

149

Travel Diary

Travel Diary

153

Travel Diary

156 — Germany, Austria, Switz.

Travel Diary

158

Germany, Austria, Switz.

Travel Diary

160

Germany, Austria, Switz.